WHY WE ARE NOT HINDUS

WHY WE ARE NOT HINDUS

Murzban Jal

Why We Are Not Hindus
Murzban Jal

First Published 2015
Reprinted 2016
Reprinted 2018

ISBN 978-93-5002-376-1 (Pb)

Published by
AAKAR BOOKS
28 E Pocket IV, Mayur Vihar Phase I
Delhi 110 091, India
aakarbooks@gmail.com
www.aakarbooks.com

Printed at
Sapra Brothers, Delhi 110 092

Contents

Acknowledgments

This book is an outcome of essays on fascism published in *Mainstream*. I would like to thank the editor Sumit Chakravartty for allowing me to let these anti-fascist essays come out in the form of a book. My thanks to everyone at the Indian Institute of Education, Pune—a social science research institute started by the legendary socialist J.P. Naik—who have inspired me to work on the burning issue of the rise of fascism in India.

Preface

This book is on political Hinduism and its role in the emergence and growth of fascism In India. The methodology that it follows is a form of Freudo-Marxism where the role played by the political and ideological superstructure is put in its historical perspective. While three of Marx's concepts are taken into consideration—alienation, reification and fetishism; concepts that are predicated on the historical materialist theory of caste domination and class struggle—two of Freud's concepts—neurosis and psychosis—are also placed at the centre of scientific analysis.

Consequently the role played by the law of repetition in producing the neurotic and psychotic elements in the political unconscious is put at the basis of this book. What this book claims is that besides the element of fear produced in the individual and collective psyche, the elements of neurosis and psychosis produced also stand central to the programme of the production of the fascist unconscious. Consequently the role played by alienation, reification and fetishism along with the role of neurosis and psychosis in producing the fascist unconscious is analyzed.

While this book appears to be a critique of religion, in actuality it is not so. It is about the use and abuse of ideas—here the ideas of "Hinduism" and "Hindutva"—their historical location and how colonialism mobilized these used and abused ideas for their colonial divide and rule policy. This book is on the critique of fascism and the historicist and humanist development of a radical secularism that actively confronts fascism. One thus makes a distinction between radical secularism and liberal secularism. The former is a Marxist theory of the annihilation of caste and the entire capitalist class system, while the latter as mere separation of state and religion is a pale imitation of Western bourgeois parliamentary democracy.

What we are claiming is that India of the elites is living on borrowed ideas. Not only are the ideas of liberal secularism and fascism borrowed ideas from the capitalist and imperialist baggage of Western Europe, but also the idea of "Hinduism" itself is a borrowed idea. We are thus plagued by these three ideas—secularism (as liberal secularism), fascism and "Hinduism". We are keeping this term "Hinduism" in what Edmund Husserl called "brackets", since we intend to unleash the radical politics of suspicion on this very term that we claim is vacuous and fuzzy, a fuzziness that the ruling nationalist and colonial elites could mobilize for their imperial rule in India.

If Marx and Freud's methodologies are used, then so is the methodology of B.R. Ambedkar's critique of the caste system and its entire ideological superstructure called "Hinduism" placed central to this book. The critique of "Hinduism" (both political and anthropological "Hinduism") is from this perspective. A note of caution is however necessary. We are not involved in a messianic secularist critique of religion. On the other hand, we are claiming that political Hinduism has emerged in modern times in the era of imperialism in permanent crisis, while anthropological Hinduism has been the culture of both pre-capitalist India and capitalism in the era of liberal democracy. V.D. Savarkar, Nathuram Godse, K.B. Hegdewar and M.S. Golwalkar belonged to the first camp, while Gandhi and Nehru belonged to the camp of liberal democracy. From the Ambedkarite perspective, as we shall see, both are wrong. According to this Ambedakarite perspective, there are things that lie deep beneath both Hinduism and Hindutva.

And in this Ambedekarite perspective, one thus, can only recall Shakespeare:

> There are more things in heaven and earth,
> Horatio,
> Than are dreamt of in your philosophy.[1]

REFERENCE

1. William Shakespeare, 'Hamlet', in *The Complete Works of William Shakespeare*, ed. V.J. Craig (London: Henry Pordes, 1983), Act. I, Scene 5, p. 950.

1

Introduction: On the Burning of Books

> If Hindu Raj becomes a reality then it would be the greatest menace to this country.
>
> *B.R. Ambedkar*

> A Klee painting named 'Angelus Novus' shows an angel looking as though he is about to move away from something he is fixedly contemplating. His eyes are staring, his mouth is open, his wings are spread. This is how one pictures the angel of history. His face is turned toward the past. Where we perceive a chain of events, he sees one single catastrophe which keeps piling wreckage and hurls it in front of his feet. The angel would like to stay, awaken the dead, and make whole what has been smashed. But a storm is blowing in from Paradise; it has got caught in his wings with such violence that the angel can no longer close them. The storm irresistibly propels him into the future to which his back is turned, while the pile of debris before him grows skyward. This storm is what we call progress.
>
> *Walter Benjamin*

The Angel of History or the Demon of Mythology?

In this book on political Hinduism and the role played by fear, neurosis and psychosis to produce the fascist unconscious, we begin with the present. Let us have a look at a quote from Subramanian Swamy, a right-wing economist, politician (he is a member of the Bharatiya Janata Party) and author of *Hindutva and National Renaissance*, *Virat Hindu Identity*, *Hindus Under Siege*,

Rama Setu: Symbol of National Unity. According to him, Indian history, as we know it, or taught by historians like Romila Thapar and Bipan Chandra is a form of a peculiar type of what he calls "pseudo-history", where secular historians appear as "British imperialists". Consider his rather remarkable insights:

> The Sarasvati River had been called mythical by historians for the last 200 years. But now with the help of laser science it has been possible to locate the Vedic river underground and has now opened it up. Dwarka, the city of Lord Krishna, was similarly declared to be mythical. But under the dynamic leadership of Dr. S.R. Rao of the Archaeological Survey of India, Dwarka city was found under the ocean of the Gujarat coast. These discoveries find no reflection in our history textbooks. The chronology that we are made to follow in history textbooks of today is such that Hindu civilization is shown to arrive after the beginnings of the Judeo-Christian civilization. Over 2,000 years of Hindu history has been truncated to zero for this purpose. Hence, just as Gandhiji started a revolution in India by urging the masses to burn British clothes, wear Khadi, and boycott British goods, we nationalists too advocate clarity with regard to our national identity by burning history books concocted by British imperialists.[1]

We have intentionally begun with Swamy and not directly with the ideologues of the Rashtriya Swayamsevak Sangh (RSS), a right-wing Hindu supremacist organization started in 1925, in order to note how fascist programming of national consciousness also appears in liberal national newspapers. His article was published in the largely left-of-centre liberal newspaper *The Hindu*. What we see is that while the ideologists of the RSS as well as their assassins are openly flexing their fascist muscles, national newspapers also publish their noxious views. While the RSS is going guns blazing on the production of their myth of the "Hindu Rashtra", their murderers are killing comrades like Govind Pansare and their liberal representatives are openly advocating forms of violence. In these attacks by the Indian fascists, there is a very clever move where the ideologists of the RSS are pushing for an aggressive political war of attrition against Indian democracy.

In this ideological war of attrition, the RSS is roping pro-American politicians like Swamy who has been lecturing on how evil secularism and communism are. The leitmotiv of this mode of right-wing thinking is on the alleged evil character of secularism and communism—a theme that is borrowed from the repertoire of the neo-con global ideology industry. For Swamy, like the RSS and the global anti-communist culture industry, both secularism and communism are out to denigrate Hinduism and then decimate it. This is the essence of the ideologues trained in the dominant American way of thinking whose hatred for the secularist and socialist project is well known.

According to his phantasmagorical imagination, the left-secular historians are "British imperialists" (see above quote). He extols people to burn history books written by secular historians. His article clearly evokes the burning of books by the Nazis. But while evoking the memory of the burning of books by the Nazis, Swamy's article also reminds us of Walter Benjamin's angel of history from his celebrated essay 'Theses on the Philosophy of History'. According to Benjamin (he is examining a painting of Paul Klee) there is a picture of the angel of history looking backwards (in history) despite being blown forward by the storm of progress. Below this angel lie ruins.

If that was Benjamin's rendering of Klee's painting, Swamy renders quite another picture. According to Swamy, the angel of Indian history (rather the *devil of manufactured Hindutva history*) is looking backwards while being blown in the same backward direction. This demon of history is also darting below towards the ruins. Now a liberal rendering of this will suggest that Swamy is free to evoke as many angels and demons of doomsday and as much hysterical melancholia where socialist and secular historians are portrayed as betraying, what the Hindutvavadis fantasize as, "Hindu history" and "Hindu people". But a more serious reading suggests that there is nothing accidental in the article that he has penned. It is a conscious experiment with untruth that he and his political fellow travellers are experimenting with. That this article appears in *The Hindu* also implies a rather sinister design on the part of neo-liberalism and the role of the liberals in being a part of the fascist project.

There are two main motifs in Swamy's article producing violent fantasies of religious nationalism: (1) that there is something called "Hindu history" (with imagined underground Vedic rivers and fantasized submerged cities) and (2) books that do not abide by this strange dictatorship of Hindutva historians should be burnt. While one could ignore this as the moaning of an apocalyptic politician, the burning of books that he advocates is a clear message that the present political disposition of creating a fascist Raj has to be taken very seriously. Remember that his suggestion follows the banning of Wendy Doniger's *The Hindus: An Alternative History*. At one level it is clear that Swamy is trying to construct something called "Hindu politics" from the cranium of the pre-independence nationalist project by making a wedge between Nehru and Vallabhbhai Patel. At that level he is trying to claim that Nehru was wrong (and feminine) and Patel was right (and masculine) and that the (masculine) BJP is the sole heir to the politics of Patel. This he is doing because he cannot find any erstwhile mass leader who could be used as an icon for his type of divisive politics. At a deeper level he is trying to popularize the politics of Hindutva and Hindu supremacy. And anyone who opposes this is said to be an agent of what he calls "British imperialists".

Clearly Swamy has no idea of either Indian history or politics. There are multiple errors in this piece. He is trying to deduce his version of Hindutva from his magic hat that has no rabbits. What jumps from his magician's hat is not real Hindutva, but it's sad and mourning ghost. Swamy the magician with the duplicate ghost then claims that he intends to work with scientific methodology. He says that "in spite of the application of science to questions of history, Nehruvian historians are refusing to update and review the materials that go into making history books". He forgets that Mahmoud Ahmadinejad, the not so celebrated ex-president of the Islamic Republic of Iran, also said almost the same thing when he claimed that advanced historical material suggests that the Nazis did not create Auschwitz and the genocide. Ahmadinejad, was trying to veil a genocide that happened in the past, Swamy is preparing for a future genocide.

Development and Hate

In this sense one claims that there is no gap between the politics of "development" as the official policy of Narendra Modi and the hate speeches of the Hindutvavadis. There is a concrete fusion of these two. For "development" that shall now enter India is the development of neo-liberal capitalism where what David Harvey calls "accumulation through dispossession" rules the roost.

What happens is that the dominant narrative of secularism and Constitutional Democracy no longer suits the political economy of neo-liberal development. Just look at Syria, Iraq, Afghanistan and one will understand what development via neo-liberalism means. Swamy and the ideology that he represents is the ideology of brute development where the popular masses of India are divided on communal lines. The politics of development do not lie outside this communal hatred. And this is because development is no longer going to be peaceful development, no longer inclusive development. The present government's FDI in the military sector is just one example of what development is going to mean.

Over two decades ago the RSS changed the image of Rama as the god who goes into self-exile in the forests, the image that Gandhi cultivated, into the bow-wielding Rama. This one must stress was not an accidental change in image. It was a conscious construction of the image of the warrior tradition that Savarkar celebrated in his *Essentials of Hindutva*. Swamy celebrates Savarkar claiming that the "Hindu fraternity" is totally distinct from "Macaulay's intellectual progenies" (meaning Nehru and the secularists). But he forgets—no one could be as faithful to the colonial project as Savarkar. In fact it must be noted that the very term "Hindutva" is a colonial creation.

For Savarkar one had to manufacture the ideology of a masculine Hindutva that was different from the feminine ahimsa-inspired ideology that so fascinated Gandhi. Remember that Savarkar was penning this little book when Mussolini was capturing power in Italy. Remember that Savarkar and M.S. Golwalkar (the second Sarsanghachalak of the RSS and the ideological guru of Modi) eulogized the Nazis. Remember that for him, as was for Golwalkar, India was a "Hindu Rashtra" driven by what they both called the "race spirit", the spirit of being members of the fictitious "Aryan race".

Thus one must remember that for both Savarkar and Golwalkar being Hindu implies being members of this fetish called the "Aryan race". Remember that for both, Hindus belong to one race and Muslims to another. Also remember that for both of them Muslims had to be purged from India, just as the Nazis purged the Jews. This is the essence of Hindutva ideology. It is not something contingent that can be simply forgotten. The BJP cannot close its eyes to this essence of Hindutva ideology. It cannot claim to be secular, democratic and inclusive. At one moment the mask of democracy and decency will have to fall off.

According to Hindutva ideologists (Savarkar and Swamy included) there is an imagined "Aryan race" that is in perpetual battle with the Muslims. As Savarkar said in *Hindu Rashtra Darshan* Hindus and Muslims are "two antagonistic nations living in India side by side". In the same work he talked of the idea of Hindu-Muslim unity as a ghost like "willow-the-wisp". Remember that the original two-nation theory that led to the balkanization of the Indian subcontinent was Savarkar's idea.

Modi is now, here and there, with broom in hand, evoking the memory of Gandhi. But at the same time Savarkar is the ghostly master puppeteer, who hated Gandhi and wanted to militarize and industrialize the Hindus, who controls Modi. Modi's spectacle of development is the realization of this militaristic industrialization.

For Savarkar Hindutva is not Hinduism, but Hindudom. His model was not merely European fascism, but also medieval Europe, especially medieval Europe's feudal idea of Christendom. There was nothing indigenous in the thinking of Savarkar or Golwalkar. Their ideas of nationhood were borrowed lock, stock and barrel from right-wing thinkers of Western Europe. If Swamy eulogizes Savarkar, this is not out of reason. Recall Savarkar's motto: *"Hinduize all politics and militarize Hindudom"*. In this sense the model state for the Hindutvavadis is Nazi Germany. But it is also Zionist Israel and strangely also the Islamic Republic of Iran that serve as their models. After all the RSS shares a lot with the Iranian clergy, especially their hatred for secularism and their great zeal for religious nationalism.

In this sense, the BJP under Modi is not merely departing from the liberal and secular legacy that we have inherited. Swamy's game plan is not merely to "underplay the contribution of Pandit Jawaharlal Nehru in India's history" as Digvijay Singh claims ("History, Battleground of Politics", *The Hindu*, October 10, 2014). It is to consciously create a militaristic version of the Indian state. It is to make Modi look like a general on battlefield taking India to the Promised Land of eternal development. The people of India need equality, liberty and fraternity. But what the RSS shall present them with is infantry, artillery and cavalry.

Look now at the sky and try sighting Benjamin's angel of history. This time the angel does not appear as an angel, nor does history appear as history. This angel of history turned into the monster of mythology is dressed in battle gear and jackboots. This is what Savarkar wanted. This is precisely what Gandhi and Nehru did not want. That is why the RSS and its rag tag army of mythologists will always hate Gandhi and Nehru. And that is precisely why they will either want to ban books or simply burn them. Fascists one must always remember cannot think, nor do they want people to think. For them burning books is a substitute to reading them.

REFERENCE

1. Subramanian Swamy, 'History and the Nationalist Project' in *The Hindu*, October, 11, 2014.

2

On Hinduism and Hindutva: Understanding the Myth of "Hindu Rashtra"

Led by our shepherds, we suddenly found ourselves in the society of freedom on the day of its internment.

Karl Marx

The name 'Hinduism' that we now use is of recent and European construction. But it is Eurocentric to assume that when Europeans made the name they made the game. 'Hinduism' (dare I use the 'H' word, and may I stop holding up my hands for mercy with quotation marks?) is, like the armadillo, part hedgehog, part tortoise.

Wendy Doniger

Hinduism as Phantasmagoria

Quite suddenly, as if from the blue, but not totally unexpectedly, shadowy figures from the BJP-led government declared India to be a Hindu nation, or to be precise what their bizarre imagination calls "Hindu Rashtra". This chapter on the theme of why, we the people of India are not Hindus, is essential about the struggle against fascism in India, especially on the war against Indian secularism being waged by the RSS which intends to install this strange and mythical "Hindu Rashtra" in India.

At one level (the level of terminology), one can claim that these right-wing politicians cannot even think in terms constituted within nationalist terms, but think through not merely borrowed, but imagined, nay hallucinated categories. Why do we say so? We say so because their very idea of "Hindu" is not a term particular to India. We say so because this idea of "Hindu" is besides being a Brahmanical counterrevolutionary term (which B.R. Ambedkar recognized) is also a colonial constructed term which divided the people of South Asia on communal lines, a division that created the nation states of India and Pakistan. In this sense, this hallucinated product of the imagination of the right-wing elites is not merely like Wendy Doniger's armadillo, part hedgehog, part tortoise.

At the outset it must be said that the word "Hindu" is not something indigenous to India. It is in fact a Persian term. And since the Indian fascists want to build their fantasy on the myth of "Hindu Rashtra", we rebuke them for their very banality. It must be understood that the original term is Persian. The Achaemenians (who ruled Iran from 559 BCE to 330 BCE) mention the people on the east of the river Sind as Hindus, whilst the Holy Book of the ancient Iranians—the *Avesta*—calls this land *Hapt-Hindûkân.*[1] The term in antiquity was geo-cultural and strictly from an Iranian point of view. The "Hindus" were what the Iranians called the people living on the eastern part of Sindh region. Later the Arabs too used this Persian term. Remember that for the Arabs, India was and still is what they call "al-Hind". This geo-cultural West Asian usage was then inserted in the readings of India, especially by Albêrûnî. Mughal rule in India continued this Persian usage, but they Indianized it. What the Persians called *Hapt-Hindûkân* became "Hindustan". In ancient India, there were no people called the "Hindus". Instead one had the "*bamanashramanam*" (the Brahmans) and the "*shramanas*" (the Buddhists and the Jains).

Origins of terms are often problematic. While one can say that this is for the term "Hindu", one can also mention the paradox of the origins of other terms. For instance, Babur the founder of what we now know as the "Mughal Dynasty" disliked the term "Mughal"—Mughal is actually the Persianized term for "Mongol". Though Babur's mother was a Chaghtai Mughal and was also the descendant of Chingiz Khan (1162-1227 CE)—of the pre-Islamic Tengri Shaman cult—for him, "mischief and devastation must always be expected from the Mughal horde".[2]

A sort of what one may call the "cunning of reason" (to borrow the German philosopher G.W.F. Hegel's term) seems to govern national identities. The cunning of reason will govern the history of India from the Persian *Hapt Hindûkân* to Hindustan. But if the ruse of reason runs through the above mentioned course, the complete destruction of reason governs the aetiology of the imagined "Hindu Rashtra". If for Babur "mischief and devastation must always be expected from the Mughal horde", then much more mischief and devastation must always be expected from the Hindu Rashtra horde. Let us see how this Hindu Rashtra horde rides on the backs of the cunning of reason.

At this juncture it must be noted that the term "Hinduism" as is being used today by the Indian elites is basically a vacuous, cunning and fuzzy term—bereft from its West Asian origins and the complex ideological struggles fought in the Indian subcontinent for the past two and a half thousand years. Its contemporary usage is an Anglicized-Brahmanical manipulated term, manipulated firstly by the colonial state in collaboration with the upper caste elites; a manipulation that was used by the same upper caste elites in independent India, and which is now being used in its most brutal communal-fascistic form by the RSS. It must be noted that the contemporary usage—both in popular usage as well as the one used by the RSS—cannot be confused with the original Persian term. Usage of this term, mainly as a single religious entity devoid of the Islamic heritage of India, was constructed by the 18th century Orientalists based on the Judeo-Christian understanding of what constitutes a religion.[3] This usage was grounded in Brahmanical imagination, based on Vedic textuality which completely erased all anti-

Brahmanical subaltern traditions. And if they were not able to completely erase these subaltern traditions, they appropriated them. But this appropriation was and is determined by Sanskritized textuality and Brahmanism. If Marxism talks of the economic base of society being the determining element in the "last resort" in history, then we say that idealized Sanskritized hermeneutics and Brahmanism in the era of capitalism become the determining elements in producing this phantasmagoria of "Hinduism".

That is why we say that there is no unified doctrine called "Hinduism". "Hinduism" as a unified doctrine is both a myth and a ritual. And if the Orientalists (especially Max Müller) imagined a unified doctrine called "Hinduism", the colonial authorities used the same to create a Hindu-Muslim zone of conflict. Instead of using the term "Hinduism", one should use the term Brahmanism especially as the dominant ideology of the upper caste Indians, since Shankara (788-820 CE) began his counterrevolution against Buddhism. And that is why we insist that the term "Hinduism" is a fetishized cloak that veils caste and class relations. Hindutva invented by V.D. Savarkar in the 1920s (when parts of Europe were being steamrolled by fascism) further cloaks caste and class relations. We thought earlier that the Indian fascists simply cannot think, because they cannot even think in original categories. Now with the Bharatiya Janata Party (the political wing of the RSS) coming to power in New Delhi, this joke has become a tragedy. Romila Thapar notices this:

> The imposing of a religious identity as the primary political identity is of course the contribution of colonial scholarship and policy and eventually found its way even into anti-colonial nationalism. The tragedy is that, after independence, we did not question these identities but retained them. Some historians and social scientists questioned them suggesting alternative identities, but they were attacked and described as Western stooges (oddly enough), anti-national and as Marxists (thought to be the worst

abuse possible)! It was not the failure of our historical imagination but the general resistance to accepting a more nuanced and accurate understanding of the past. The methods and arguments used by religious "nationalisms" in India are rooted in colonial perceptions and procedures and will flourish as long as we accept these. We haven't even excised those colonial laws that are harmful to democracy—we continue to be governed by them.[4]

It is here that we need to bring in Walter Benjamin. Consider Benjamin:

> There is no document of civilization which is not at the same time a document of barbarism. And just as such a document is not free of barbarism, barbarism taints also the manner in which it was transmitted from one owner to another. A historical materialist therefore dissociates himself from it as far as possible. He regards it as his task to brush history against the grain.[5]

And since what one thought to be a joke, namely that some fantasy called "Hindutva" has not merely become a reality, albeit a reality in barbaric tragi-comic form, we say that not only is this fascist project of "Hindutva" a barbaric tragi-comic fiction-fantasy, but we also say that the entire project of Hinduism is a phantasmagorical project. While we are taking this theme of Hinduism as phantasmagoria, we are claiming that the term "phantasmagoria" is a central Marxist idea that Marx highlights, mainly in *Capital*, Vol. I. Phantasmagoria implies something magical, ghostly and eerie, an idea that was also central to Mary Shelley's *Frankenstein*.

What has now happened with the coming to power of the brigand of the RSS, the storm-trooper Narendra Modi as the Prime Minister of India is the activation of the phantasmagorical-Frankenstein idea. The fact is that this triumph of fascism is rooted in capitalism and the tremendous crisis that accompanies it. One thus links this idea of Hindutva as phantasmagoria with Marx's original formulation of the fetishistic and phantasmagorical character of commodity production. Read the following quote from Marx. But substitute the word "commodity" with "Hindutva" and understand how in the era of generalized commodity production, the fascist project of Hindutva has become a commodity (albeit a lethal commodity marketed by the Culture Industry of the corporate sector backing Modi) to be consumed by the masses. According to Marx:

> A commodity appears as, at first sight, a very trivial thing, and easily understood. Its analysis shows that it is in reality, a very queer thing, abounding in metaphysical subtleties and theological niceties. So far as it is value in use, there is nothing mysterious about it.....But, so soon as it steps forth as a commodity, it is changed into something transcendent. It not only stands with its feet on the ground, but, in relation to all other commodities, it stands on its head, and evolves out of its wooden brain grotesque ideas, far more wonderful than "table-turning" ever was.[6]

A brief note on the above passage is necessary, especially when we realize that practising leftists in India rather discounted Marx's original idea of the fetish character of commodities and the type of reified consciousness emerging thereon. What we are doing is putting the character of the fetish character of culture dominated by elites central to our repertoire. What we are saying is that for the elites culture is a commodity and a spectacle, while for the masses culture is an expression of their social relations of production.

Now erase the word "commodity" from the above quote of Marx and insert the word "Hindu Rashtra".

> The "Hindu Rashtra" appears as, at first sight, a very trivial thing, and easily understood. Its analysis shows that it is in reality, a very queer thing, abounding in metaphysical subtleties and theological niceties. So far as it is value in use, there is nothing mysterious about it.....But, so soon as the "Hindu Rashtra" steps forth as a commodity, it is changed into something transcendent. This "Hindu Rashtra" not only stands with its feet on the ground, but, in relation to all other commodities, it stands on its head, and evolves out of its wooden brain grotesque ideas, far more wonderful than "table-turning" ever was.

Note that the ideas of magic and ghosts are central to both the quoted passages—on the fetish character of commodities as well as that of the "Hindu Rashtra". What has happened is that a terrible inversion and distortion has happened with the coming of capitalism, such that real people have become predicates of alien life-forces. What we get from the above passage is the understanding that religious nationalism appears as a possessing force that haunts and enslaves the masses. In *Capital*, Vol. III Marx further evolves this idea and says that real actors of capitalist history are the strange pair: Monsieur Capital and Madame Rent, who are doing their ghost-walk all over the globe,[7] while humanity is destroyed by this spectral-ghost walk. What the RSS have done in India is that they have draped Monsieur Capital and Madame Rent with saffron flags.

One knows that this idea of fetishism and reification was kept central to the entire repertoire of Marx, later taken by Georg Lukács' *History and Class Consciousness*, but an idea that has been totally forgotten in the real politics of Revolutionary Marxism. While one could point out that this idea was discounted since the times of the Second International, especially by the betrayal of the revolutionary traditions of Marxism (mainly by Karl Kautsky and Georgi Plekhanov), its complete obliteration began with the Stalinist counterrevolution, when Marxism in the Soviet Union was transfigured from historicism and humanism to a form of positivism (inspired by Nicolai Bukharin) and then into bland theology (as best exemplified by Stalin's works especially in his *Economic Problems of Socialism in the USSR*). What the Established Left in India did was that it took more from Bukharin and Stalin and completely forgot the emancipatory character of Marx's humanism. And it is this vacuum that the fascists have occupied.

What happens with this above reading is that this idea of the fetishism of commodities is transformed into the fetishism of religious nationalism, especially the fetishistic attachment to religious nationalist discourses. Consider the above quote and relate it with the storm-troopers of the Indian variant of fascism. See how one now reads the fantasy of the "Hindu Rashtra" appearing at surface level as a "very trivial thing, and easily understood", while its "analysis shows that it is in reality, a very queer thing, abounding in metaphysical subtleties and theological niceties". Note how this imagined "Hindu Rashtra" as "soon as it steps forth as a commodity, it is changed into something transcendent. It not only stands with its feet on the ground, but, in relation to all other commodities, it stands on its head, and evolves out of its wooden brain grotesque ideas, far more wonderful than "table-turning" ever was". "Table-turning", in this passage of Marx refers to the craze that had gripped bourgeois Europe where the lords and the ladies evoked the spirits of the dead. A very small note on translation is necessary. First the English rendering is "table-turning", when in actually it is *making heads dance* (*"aus freien Stücken zu tanzen begänne"*)[8]. In the original German Marx says: *"Man erinnert sich, das China und die Tische su tanzen anfigen, als alle üübrige Welt still zu stehn schien—pour encourager les autres"* implying that "One may recall that China and the tables began to dance when the rest of the world appeared to be standing still."[9]

One must note that the idea of standing on its head is also reminiscent of yoga and the fetish character of the theological nationalists who since 1857 created nationalist fantasies. What we get from this passage is that the fetish character of the "Hindu Rashtra" is able to conjure more ghosts than those evoked by the traditional ghost seekers. Further the idea of the "wooden heads" of Monsieur Capital and Madame Rent fits in well with the new leaders of India. The "grotesque ideas" that emerge from their wooden heads are the ideas of the racist and supremacist ideology of the imagined "Hindu race". And it is with these grotesque ideas emerging from the fascists' wooden heads that one notes how the liberal-democratic state that stands on its head with the dancing tables, planchets and the spirits of the long dead is now evolving into the fascist Hindutva state. One had earlier heard how apes evolved into humans. Now we hear how liberals have evolved into fascists. And central to this very strange type of evolution, stands the political state, a problem that the Established Left never understood. Why do we say so? We say so, because communism which should never have taken the route of the state, finally did become statist. Not only was Stalin wrong here, but also revolutionaries like Trotsky and Bukharin were wrong in trying to postulate an idea of a "socialist state".

What we are saying is that Revolutionary Marxism does not take the role of state-socialism. Thus when one critiques the fascist myth of the Hindu Rashtra one does not advocate a form of liberal secularism, with its idea of the separation of state and religion. Instead Revolutionary Marxism attacks the ruling classes and the political elites by pointing out that the state is not the terrain of class-neutrality, but the engine of class despotism, where the state shows that its only role is managing class order.

What happened in India was that the Established Left—led by the CPI(M)—did not understand this process thus making them a part of the state that they were supposed to destroy. But this was only one part. With the development of capitalism in India and with the onslaught of neo-liberal capitalism (a process started by the Congress) the state was taken over by the RSS first led by the alleged liberal Atal Bihari Vajpayee (from 1998-2004) and now in May 2014 by Narendra Modi. This has led to the transformation of the liberal state into the fascist state. The tragedy is that what one once thought was a comedy scripted in this crazy text called *Essentials of Hindutva* written by Savarkar in 1921-22 has become a reality.

So what is wrong with this text that one calls phantasmagorical and Frankensteinean? And why does one say that this idea is outrightly racist, casteist and fascistic and the contemporary Indian state armed with this bizarre political ideology of Hindutva will lead to the same sort of horrors that other fascists states experienced?

On the Barbaric Tragi-comedy called "Hindutva"

Let us have a look at it. In this work *Essentials of Hindutva* Savarkar outlines a mythical imagined history (in the form of social myth that the German Nazis had invoked) of India, beginning with the Orientalist myth of the Aryans (his eulogization of the warrior-priest tradition of Vedic times), the rise and fall of Buddhism in India (for Savarkar the Buddhist ideas of ahimsa and universal brotherhood—he calls them "opiates"—were signs of weakness where what he calls the "political virility" and the "manly nobility of our race" ended) and the consequent triumph of the Vedic warrior-priestly tradition with the fall of the Mauryan empire.[10] What must be recognized that while there are traces of Nietzsche, the central idea of the *Essentials of Hindutva* is the Nazi idea of the Aryan race in perpetual war with other races. And for Savarkar's mythical-history, Buddhism collapsed because it digressed from the warrior practice of his imagined Aryan race only to preach and practise what he calls the "mumbos and jumbos of universal brotherhood".[11]

For him "so long as India had to live at all a life whether spiritual or political according to the right of her soul, she must not lose the strength of national and racial cohesion". One should not forget not only the racist but also the casteist underpinnings of Savarkar where nationality is defined not only by what was known to bourgeois nationalists as "common culture and common language", but primarily as "common blood". The imperialist and racist thoughts are obvious: "If the earth is conquered by the Mlecchas this land of the gods will perish, because of the abolishing of sacrifices and other religious rites." One should not forget that the idea of the "Indian nation" for Savarkar is based on imperialist conquest where Shalivahan, the grandson of Vikramaditya "conquered the irresistible

Shakas, the Chinese, the Tartars, the Balhikas, Kamrupas, Romans, Khorajas and Shathas".

What the initial idea of Indian fascism under Savarkar did was that it reinvented the idea of the Indian people as some sort of homogeneous people who are determined in the last resort by the fascist idea of blood descent. And what this imagined homogeneity did was that it then recreated a false collective in the form of a communitarian idea of society. But what this idea of Indian fascism did was that it constructed a spurious idea of communitarianism, or what one could call "estrangement communitarianism" where neither equality nor liberty exists. Here the modern national popular unity is disrupted for a fascist idea of the "people", where this false collectivity firstly erases the idea of social classes for the idea of a national whole. It was Mussolini (the father of Italian fascism, and also an ex-socialist) who said that the idea of classes and class struggle was false. Instead it was the idea of the national that would be the essence of Italian fascism. One also knows that this idea of the "people" (*Volk*) was the essence of German fascism based on the ideology of blood descent where the idea of citizenship was displaced for an idea of "community" (*Gemeinschaft*). That is why it is important to note that community and citizenship "have had a problematic relationship", as has been recently pointed out, "since the origins of political thought. The Greeks had only one word to express these two aspects: *politeia*, whence we derive our 'politics' as well as our 'police'".[12]

What classical fascism in Europe did was that it removed the ideas of citizenship or politics proper and inserted the ideas of community and police. It also invented the right-wing ideology of race. The Indian fascists then inserted a colonial borrowing of race theory wherein they made claims of the "Race spirit" in the 1920s. The 'Aryan'/'Jew' opposition was changed into the 'Hindu'/'Muslim' opposition. If Savarkar initiated this idea in the early 1920s, the RSS would make this into a doctrine in the late 1930s. M.S. Golwalkar's *We, or Our Nation Defined* is the second master text of Indian fascism after Savarkar's *Hindutva*. We noted what Savarkar said. Now consider Golwalkar:

> The foreign races in Hindustan must either adopt Hindu culture and language, must hold to respect and hold in reverence the Hindu religion, must entertain no idea but those of the glorification of the Hindu religion and lose their separate existence, to merge in the Hindu race, or may stay in the country, wholly subordinated to the Hindu nation, claiming nothing, deserving no privileges, far less any preferential treatment—not even citizen's rights.[13]

Consider two more statements of Indian fascism. The first is from *We, or Our Nation Defined* and the second from Savarkar's *Hindu Rashtra Darshan*. This is what Golwalkar says: "Race is the body of the nation, and that with its fall, the nation, ceases to exist." And now note the shocking statement of Savarkar: "Nazism provided undeniably the saviour of Germany". It is noting these two absolutely fascistic statements that one is now compelled to ask: "What did this fictitious "Race spirit" now drunk on the Aryan-Hindu fantasy talk of?" It talked of the "Hindu nation" based on the imagined "Hindu race". Now it is well known that it was Savarkar's *Essentials of Hindutva* where the ideology of Hindutva was invented as a racist political ideology where the categories "Hinduness", and "Hindudom" were created borrowed totally from European feudalism's idea of "Christendom". That is why it is important to say that these ideas of "Hinduness", and "Hindudom" came into the lexicon of the Indian fascist movement from fascist Europe. *In no way can one claim that the idea of Hindutva is indigenous to Indian civilization*. If the brutal form emerged from European fascism, the early Romantic version, especially as found in the works of Novalis and Friedrich Schlegel was also latently present in its ideological cranium. Consider Novalis's 1799 work *Christianity or Europe*:

> Those were beautiful, magnificent times, when Europe was a Christian land, when one Christianity dwelled on this civilized continent, and when one common interest joined the most distant provinces of this vast spiritual empire without great worldly possessions one sovereign governed and unified the great political force. Immediately under him stood one enormous guild, open to all, executing his every wish and zealously striving to consolidate his beneficent power. Every member of this society was honoured everywhere. If the common people sought from their clergyman comfort or help, protection or advice, gladly caring for his various needs in return, he also gained protection, respect and audience from his superiors. Everyone saw these elect men, armed with miraculous powers, as the children of heaven, whose mere presence and affection dispensed all kinds of blessings. Childlike faith bound the people to their teachings. How happily everyone could complete their earthly labours, since these holy men had safeguarded them a future life, forgave every sin, explained and erased every blackspot in this life. They were the experienced pilots on the great uncharted seas, in whose shelter one could scorn all storms, and whom one could trust to reach and land safely on the shores of the real paternal world. The wildest and most voracious appetites had to yield with honour and obedience to their words. Peace emanated from them. They preached nothing but love for the holy, beautiful lady of Christianity who, endowed with divine power, was ready to rescue every believer from the most terrible dangers.[14]

What Savarkar did was that he took the Romantic idea of nationalism bereft of its modern and aesthetical sensibility. While Savarkar's work smacks of the unacknowledged borrowings from Novalis and Schlegel on the Romantic idea of nationalism, he most certainly cannot be compared to either of them. For Novalis and Schlegel the ideas of beauty and liberty stood central to their works. For them the political state had to be formed around the idea of beauty. The European Romantics wanted a unity of politics, aesthetics and religion. Savarkar created the absolute identity between politics and racial-religion. What he did was that he politicized, in the right-wing sense, religious prejudices and transformed these into the ideology of racial superiority. But what he primarily did was he *feudalized Indian nationhood*—in fact feudalized it in a very Catholic Church type (and thus papal type) borrowed from feudal Europe. Thus what he did was transform feudal Europe's idea of Christendom into the idea of Hindudom. Strictly speaking Hindudom is a total fiction. It has never existed, just as no "Hindu Church" ever existed. Savarkar continuously talked in *Essentials of Hindutva* of a "Buddhist Church". What Savarkar did was that he created a fantasy of "Hindutva" borrowed totally from the lens of feudal Europe. What Golwalkar and the RSS did was *transform this fantasy into a phantasmagoria*. Hindutva since Golwalkar was possessed by the spirits of the long dead. And just as commodities seized by these spirits (as in Marx's *Capital*) began to dance, so too Hindutva since the early 1930s did their ghostly dancing. See one concrete fascistic ghost dancing which is said to be essentially imperialist (as one European proponent of Hinduism and Nazism once said): where "Hinduism, once, used to extend over what is now Afghanistan, over Java, over Cambodia. Powerful Hindu India could reconquer these lands and give them back the pride of their Indian civilization. She could make Greater India".[15] One has to note that this idea of "Greater India" or "Akhand Bharat" is essentially a European fascist invention.

If European fascism gave sanction to this idea of imperial India, it was in actuality the Orientalists who since the middle of the 18th century were producing this fantasy. And if the seeds were sown by the Orientalists, the plant that grew was watered and nurtured by the Hindu reform movement and nationalist leaders with the help of the newly founded Indian universities. In 1926 the Greater India Society was founded in Calcutta in order to study the history and culture of Asia. Even Rabindranath Tagore with his idealized-Sanskritized reformism found a place at this Greater India Society as its spiritual head (*purodhā*). R.C. Mazumdar as the general editor of the voluminous *History and Culture of the Indian People* was a prominent contributor to the production of this form of primordial Hindu nationalism. This methodology of imagined nationalism was not merely flawed. It was based on European chronology: ancient history, medieval, modern. The consequent and very contemporary production of the "Hindu Rashtra" is predicated on this little history just outlined.

What one needs to do is to relate this imagined nationalist history along with these fantasies and phantasmagorias of the "Hindu Rashtra" with the modern idea of democracy where the ideas of liberty, equality and fraternity are proudly displayed on its banners. One should also emphasize how Ambedkar repeatedly claimed that this triad of democracy was not possible under Hinduism. If authentic democracy was not possible under Hinduism, under Hindutva the democratic ideas of liberty, equality and fraternity would soon be transformed into the bourgeois reality of infantry, artillery and cavalry.

The bourgeois state in its liberal stage was fascinated by liberty; in its fascist stage it is artillery that would fascinate it. The Indian liberals would herald the welfare state; their fascist descendants would unleash the warfare state. And in this ecstatic evolution from liberty to artillery, the Established Left would be dumbfounded. They thought that they would take refuge in the state. But neither Savarkar nor Modi would give them refuge.

The State and Counterrevolution

That is why we say that theories of the state, both classical and modern, stand on both rigorous and shaky grounds. This ironical situation is because the state is predicated on conflicting and warring classes and consequently represents the interests of only the dominant classes. Two main motifs emerge from theories of the state, one that the state stands for the public good and is the embodiment of morality. Aristotle's *Politics* and Hegel's *Philosophy of Right* are the best examples of this idea of the state. The exact opposite emerges from the philosophy of Marx, namely that the state is nothing but the managing committee of the ruling classes and the modern state the managing committee of the global bourgeoisie[16]. For Marx, then the public good stands *outside* the realm of the state. If Hegel thought that the state was the embodiment of the moral good, for Marx it was the embodiment of the immoral evil. Thus for Marx one had to transcend the realm of the state for the possibilities of the realization of this moral good. Yet a sort of tragedy struck Marxism with Stalin's counterrevolution against the Bolsheviks. What happened in Soviet Marxism was that Marxism was made to stand on its head, where the counterrevolution against Marxism spoke strangely in the name of Marx. One did not have merely a duplicate Marx, but an inverted Marx. And this inverted Marx would not only haunt the whole world, it would stalk it. India would be no exception.

If tragedy struck the Marxist movement for human emancipation where state capitalism would turn out to be its goal; modern India was likewise struck by a new tragedy, the definite sign being the acceptance of the American-led ideologies and economic policies of neo-liberal capitalism in the early 1990s. What this American-led neo-liberalism did was attack not only the ideological foundations of social democracy. It would also attack the ideology of secularism, in order to construct a neo-conservative and anti-secular agenda for India.

However this "post-socialist" age would give way not to the neo-liberal fantasy of making the whole world in the image of capitalism. Multiple contradictions would emerge where the Congress Party that held all the contradictions of India in its own fold, would now burst in multiple contradictions. The most dominant image emerging in this "post-Soviet" age would be the communal image of the Hindutva right. And with it the destruction of the historical Babri Mosque in 1992 by right-wing extremists, followed by the seizure of political power in New Delhi by the BJP, an ideology emerged that did not merely differ from that of Constitutional Democracy, but sought to destroy this very democracy. What they did was launch a war of attrition on Indian Constitutional Democracy, where they dug trenches in Indian democracy and put their ideological paratroopers in these political trenches.

The Indian state, so we learnt from the early 1990s, had to be a "Hindu state" governed by the ideology of "Hindutva", where Indian ideology was no longer determined by the idea of citizenship, but by the idea of nationalist biological descent. Consequently racist ideology supplemented democratic ideology. The Indian heritage and Indian ideology soon mimicked the ideologies of Nazi Germany and Zionist Israel. Yet as we learn from Perry Anderson's *The Indian Ideology* that this fantasy of the "Hindu state" grew in the cranium of the Indian national movement itself, with Gandhi being a proponent of this fantasy. What we learn thus is that liberal democracy in India did not exclude the right-wing idea of this "Hindu state".

So how does one refigure the political philosophies of human emancipation, especially when liberal democracy has been promoting Narendra Modi (the genocidical overlord of Gujarat who oversaw the 2002 anti-Muslim pogrom) as the glorious Prime Minister of India? And sadly when liberal democracy did achieve its aims of putting the Gujarat satrap as the Prime Minister in May 2014, the brutality, incompetence and impotence of liberalism comes to the fore. And with the new government that is actively promoting its fascist Hindutva agenda, and both the liberals and the Stalinists totally bewildered by the triumph of fascism, the philosophy of emancipation that Marx first drew in his *On the Jewish Question* (where humanity would be freed from the brutality of semi-feudalism, capitalism and the state) would gain greater importance.

One possible answer to this question of human emancipation and the critique of not only the fascist project of Hindutva, but also the critique of Hinduism as such, comes from the Radical Left and Dalit movement which confronts the phantasmagoric idea of the "Hindu state", by claiming that one needs to deconstruct the very idea of Indian ideology as "Hindu ideology". One knows that besides the works of Jyotiba Phule, Periyar and B.R. Ambedkar who had all launched wars of position against this phantasmagorical 'Hindu' ideology, it was the great Indian historians starting with D.D. Kosambi, R.S. Sharma and Romila Thapar who questioned this 'Hinduism' itself, claiming that Hinduism was basically a class-caste ideology determined by the ruling elites and in no way could be reduced to the culture of the popular masses. It is by putting this "Hinduism" under the hermeneutics of suspicion that the radical democratic movement in India would be able to redefine itself. One recalls Kancha Ilaiah here: who says: "Now in your own interest and in the interest of this great country you must learn to listen and to read what we say. A people who refuse to listen to new questions and learn new answers will perish and not prosper".[17] And with the RSS in charge of the Indian state, one is sure that the fascist elites refuse to listen to new questions and learn new answers. When and how they will perish remains to be seen. But this perishing, as we know at least since Gramsci is to be carried out as a philosophy of praxis, or to recall Lenin as aesthetical insurrection.

And it is in this site of learning the art of insurrection (that one learns from Lenin) that one talks of the details of the Revolutionary Marxist idea of the state as inherently anti-democratic and how the proletariat revolution as heralding human emancipation by abolishing all forms of exploitation is perfected. But how would this political movement of the proletarian revolution and the cultural movement for human emancipation relate to the Marxist question of socialism, especially how human emancipation defined as class-caste-gender emancipation relates itself to the classical Marxist question of the dictatorship of the proletariat? Would this idea of the dictatorship of the proletariat be an aberration from the democratic ideals or should one read this idea as the realization of direct democracy?

Probably due to lack of study of historical materialist dialectics, the Marxist theory of the state, especially the question of the dictatorship of the proletariat has not been sufficiently understood. And also because the Stalinist counterrevolution pretended to be a form of an authentic Marxism, and also because the counterrevolutionary Soviet state since 1928 that was built on the political economy of state capitalism and the political idea of the Oriental despot, the question of the dictatorship of the proletariat, and following it the Marxist theory of state and radical democracy were left totally opaque and misunderstood. It was forgotten that for Marx, there is no state in communism (even in the first stage of communism, the so-called lower stage as he called it in his *Critique of the Gotha Programme*). The state, for Marx has to be smashed[18], this smashing that is not replaced with another form of state, but what one calls the "anti-state". What then is this anti-state and how does real democracy appear on the scene of real history? While it has been recognized that Marx insisted on a political logic of historicism and humanism where it were always the masses that make history and no substitute could replace the working masses, it seems that post-Marx-Marxism had blundered where the finger of suspicion went to Lenin, who seemingly replaced Marx's humanism with a brutal form of socialist dictatorship.

This of course is incorrect. Consider Lenin's political logic where revolutionary seizure of power is said to be based on the initiative of the "people from below",[19] where "the source of power is not a law enacted by parliament", but on the "direct rule of the people".[20] The Republic of Soviets of Workers', Agricultural Labourers' and Peasants' Deputies is contrasted to the rule of the police, army and the bureaucracy.[21] Lenin thus recognizes two distinct forms of power: the bourgeois "centralized power" and the "direct initiative of the people from below."[22] What Engels called the *Gemeinwesen*[23] is literally the rule of what we know now as the rule of the "commons", where the abolishment of private property and the state with the abolishment of commodity production is the *sine qua non* of revolutionary politics.

A Brief Note on the Alienated Signifier Called "Hinduism"

This book that argues for the impossibility of being a Hindu, while picking up the theme of Kancha Ilaiah's work *Why I Am Not a Hindu* far transcends his work by a historical materialist analysis of the entire contemporary discourse of Hinduism. Consequently this book is actually an investigation of not only the cultural politics in contemporary India and how the RSS fascist brigade is decimating the liberal Congress Party and then attacking the Left and the entire democratic tradition in India, but is also an actual critique of the political economy of neo-liberal capitalism. It is thus, at the same time, a political attack on the proponents of Hindutva. But it is also an attack on liberal democracy and the Indian variant of liberal democracy. It is thus also an attack on the liberal democrats. Firstly we must agree with Lenin and Žižek by claiming that liberalism is not the home for democracy.[24]

After stating the insufficiency of liberalism and the inability to handle the contradictions of the present epoch that we identify as the era of late imperialism in permanent crisis, we move to the question of religion, namely the question of Hinduism that Ambedkar had critiqued as a form of anti-humanism. But how does one concretize this critique of Hinduism as anti-humanism in radical politics? And since we have been told by the political right in India that the Indian state ought to be a "Hindu state", we are concretely setting the agenda of revolutionary politics to understand the possible alternatives to not only the fascism of the Hindutva Parivar, but also the politics of liberal democracy that is itself nurturing this form of fascism. Our concern is democracy and by democracy we mean *real democracy*, not formal democracy that parliamentary democracy advocates.

One begins with a sort of confession. For in saying that it is impossible to be a Hindu, one could be said to be implying that a type of confusion reigns where the borders of the descriptive, explanatory and the normative are set up. After all if borders are the essence of all class societies, they are the Essence (with a capital "E") of Indian caste society. Borders, in fact what Etienne Balibar has called the "borders of cruelty", become a type of a Hegelian *Wesen* that is so deeply ingrained in Indian society that to imagine a casteless society seems to be improbable. It is our concern to turn this improbable into the probable and to link the Marxist philosophy of the dictatorship of the proletariat with the very important idea of annihilation of caste.

Despite these deep-rooted borders whereby the fascists have dug deeper trenches into the political life-world with the political signboard that reads "Hindutva", we insist that: *it is impossible to be a Hindu!* We do not say: "Why we ought not to be Hindus". We do not intend to insert a Kantian norm of the metaphysical "ought" onto reality. On the contrary, one is trying to stretch the possibilities of Marxist science of historical materialism into the social and political life-world of modern India where the Indian subaltern thinkers, especially Jyotiba Phule and B.R. Ambedkar, along with Freud, form the basis of our theory of radical democracy.

Unlike the form of historical materialism sanctified by the Stalinist counterrevolution which worked in a bland form of metaphysical positivism, our understanding of historical materialism is to rethink it as a "Revolution with a Revolution". One knows that this term of Robespierre is recalled presently by Žižek. One also knows that it evokes a certain form of radicalism where Gramsci's philosophy of praxis is reworked in the context of the understanding of social formations in India, especially the context of the caste question. Not only will the caste question be part of our discourse, but also the critique of the Indian nation state that was built on the inherent communal Brahmanical ideas of a re-worked neo-Hinduism.

It must be noted that by "Hinduism" we imply the very concrete context that Ambedkar worked in. While our understanding is built on rigorous forms of Revolutionary Marxism, we will also be involving what we call a "Freudo-Marxist-Ambedkarite" understanding of social formation and the role of the Indian liberal state. In this sense we are revisiting the sites of radical praxis—of a reinvention of a radical left in the age of neo-liberalism. Again in more than one sense we are revisiting the sites of extremely serious social sciences and revolutionary politics, a seriousness where the voice of radical subalternism of what I call "Marxist-Ambedkarism" is heard. This form of "Marxist-Ambedkarism" firstly relates Indian society in terms of caste-class and then brings in the Leninist idea of learning insurrection as art. Unlike the Established Left in India that has by and large ignored the caste question (or simply has not been able to understand it largely because it could not understand Marx's idea of multilinear history where caste, based on the theory of the Asiatic mode of production was Marx's main idea of Indian history) and also unlike the Established Left that has operated at the level of the state, forgetting Marx's dictum on the smashing of the state, we take this idea of multilinear history with caste-class as its basis and also take Marx's anti-state understanding of radical politics. This brings us to the first of our propositions: there can be no real revolution without a Cultural Revolution where the old anti-humanist morality determined by the class-caste system is transcended. In a very Ambedkarite sense it also means that this needs a transcendence of not only the caste system with its absolutely outdated sense of morals, but needs a transcendence of what one calls "Hinduism" itself. When we are using the terms "Hindus" and "Hinduism", we are using it in the Ambedkarite dialectical perspective.

Hinduism, as we know it since the last century, has two

main motifs:

(1) The Sanskritized version one that originated in Brahmanical society, but whose imagination largely developed from a type of Romantic idealism that began possible with William Jones and perfected by Max Müller, a motif that culminated in Gandhi and Nehru, and

(2) the right-wing sense that began with Bankim Chandra which culminated in the discourses of Hindutva.

Unfortunately the folk tradition that resisted Brahmanism for centuries, has since independence been submerged by these two discourses. "Hinduism", as we know it today, is a kitsch of these two types of discourses: the Romantic and the fascist. The Brahmanical base will remain at the core of both these versions. Origins are always said to be problematic, yet the origins of Hinduism lie in the 10th mandala of the *Rg Veda* where a certain form, of not only class and race-based stratification, but also a form of schizophrenia was written on its banners. And since we have been told, more than once by the established order of things, that "we", the "we" that comprises the Indian nation state is basically the "we-ness" of Hinduism, the "we-ness" that is said to lie as the metaphysical basis of so-called "Indian civilization", we turn once more to the seriousness of both social sciences as well as to the site of radical praxis that seeks to overthrow this "we-ness" of the class-caste system along with its inherent racism and schizophrenia. If the Indian collective is said to be a "Hindu collective", then it is truly a false collective, a collective that refuses to think. Consider the foundational myth of both caste-stratification as well as Hinduism where the Brahmans are said to be the mouth while the other soçial groups are said to be the arms, thighs, feet and other unmentioned parts. The foundational myth does not talk of the brain or the heart. It thus does not (and cannot) talk of thinking and feeling. Take this case and relate it with Ambedkar's radical thesis of a Cultural Revolution not only against the social structures of caste-stratification, but also against the system called "Hinduism" that protects and nurtures not only this form of stratification, but all forms of stratification and all forms of regressive thinking.

The point therefore is to study the false sense of the "Hindu collective" that makes impossible the construction of an "Indian collective", a true collective where the unity of the popular classes is possible. It is also a critique of this false sense of Indian liberalism, especially on the parliamentary system that protects and nurtures this false collective. In this sense we agree with another observation of Žižek who claims that "fidelity to the democratic consensus means the acceptance of the present liberal-parliamentary consensus, which precludes any serious questioning of how this liberal-democratic order is complicit in the phenomena it officially condemns and, of course, any serious attempt to imagine a society whose socio-political order would be different".[25]

Imagining the world whose socio-political order would be different is also to imagine the repoliticization of the world by what Antonio Negri after Marco Revelli calls the "New Militants".[26] Who then are these New Militants and what do they do? What is their relation to Marx's proletariat and Ambedkar's annihilators of caste? How does this proletariat-multitude become the New Militants? What do they do with the metaphysics of Indian civilization and how do they create the New Physics of the "commons"—a radical New Space—which dissolves the old structures of caste-stratification? One has to construct these New Spaces. One critiques liberalism and argues for a different form of Radical Left politics which operates neither in the spaces of civil society nor the state. Instead it argues for the struggle being carried out in the space of the "commons", the "commons" where liberty, equality and fraternity (or "equa-liberty" as Balibar calls it) unleashes its attack on the caste-class system, a system where classes are said to be "trapped in castes".[27]

Hinduism as the Symptom-Fetish of Human Alienation in India

How Hinduism becomes firstly a construct in modern India created by the colonial state with help of the Brahmanical collaborators which then becomes a symptom-fetish of an underlying anti-democratic bourgeois social system is what one needs to explore. In Marxist historical materialist terms one says that human alienation in everyday life is the basis of this modern construct of Hinduism, while the contemporary discourse of Hinduism as the *projected lack* is the superstructure of this alienation. But what is most important is how Hinduism as this projected lack of alienation has become a central category that has literally gripped the Indian masses. In the late 1850s (after the defeat of the First Revolutionary War of Independence) Hinduism was a category mobilized to garner some sort of self-esteem against the defeat of the Revolution, later to become the mass psychology of the Indian freedom movement. That this mass psychology of Hinduism has now become the mass psychology of fascism as Hindutva is something that should concern us. What one needs to state is that while the symptom-fetish is a phantasmagorical mode of appearance of a concealed social structure (of human alienation), it has also a life of its own.

This is because this symptom-fetish called "Hinduism" is similar to the value form that Marx outlines in *Capital* where the process of metamorphosis of commodities determined by the trio: alienation (implying the loss of the self)-reification (meaning a form of "thingfication" or the dehumanization of humanity)-fetishism (or the succumbing of humanity to this monstrous thing) rules the roost not only in market economies, but also in the ideological practices of post-colonial nation states. We say that in the production of commodities there is a loss of human and material form and the production of a dubious double where a type of monstrous machine is produced that itself creates another double that Marx calls the "ghost"[28]. So we have two dubious doubles: the monstrous machine and the ghost in commodities. But we also have the same dubious double appearing in the production of the commodity called "Hinduism".

And it is in this site that one needs to state how this *dubious double* emerges on the scene of history, claiming to be the original. While we have taken this idea of the *double* from Freud's *The Uncanny*, we can also relate this with the idea of *duplication* that Marx drew in his *Theses on Feuerbach*. What happens is that this double-duplicate creates not merely an imaginary world, but a totally deluded world, which totally veils the real world.[29] To understand this process of creation of the dubious double and the consequent psychotic veiling and forgetfulness of reality which is the fundamental methodological core that Marx outlines in the *Economic and Philosophic Manuscripts of 1844* and *Capital* one has also to understand the psychoanalytic methodology that Freud drew in his *Interpretation of Dreams*. In the *Interpretation of Dreams*, Freud says how the censorship mechanism works where the latent structure goes through a process of repression and consequent censorship, thus projecting a duplicate surface structure. In India the entire discourse of repression and censorship called "Hinduism" appears as this deluded surface structure.

What we are doing (as stated in the above paragraph) is now relating this process of the duplicate with the problematic of alienation and the consequent process of metamorphosis. In *Capital* we see how humans are changed into things (commodities to be precise). Now what we need to do is relate this metamorphosis of humans into things with Žižek's idea of the digestive system[30], but a digestive system gone totally wrong, where, in the production of commodities one has actually a process of shitting. Thus in *Capital* we see how people shit commodities. The accumulation of capital is actually an accumulation of shit. We have now "the rise of 'dead nature'".[31] "Accumulate, accumulate! That is Moses and the prophets!"[32], as Marx said in the third volume of *Capital*, becomes: "Shit, shit, this is the essence of both bourgeois political economy and fascist political theology".

REFERENCES

1. See the Zoroastrian *Pahlavi Vendidâd* (Zand=Î Jvît-Dêv=Dât), transliteration and translation by B.T. Anklesaria (Mumbai: K.R. Cama Oriental Institute, 2002), p. 12.
2. Zahir Uddin Muhammad Babur, *Babur Nama*, ed. Dilip Hiro (London: Penguin Books, 2006).
3. See Richard King, *Orientalism and the Myth of Modern Hinduism* (New Delhi: Critical Quest, 2008), p. 10.
4. Praveen Swamy, Interview of Romila Thapar, 'Ideas of History', in *The Hindu*, April 5, 2014.
5. Walter Benjamin, 'Theses on the Philosophy of History', in *Illuminations*, trans Harry Zohn (Glasgow: Fontana/Collins, 1979), p. 258.
6. Karl Marx, *Capital*, Vol. I (Moscow: Progress Publishers, 1983), p. 76.
7. Karl Marx, *Capital*, Vol. III (Moscow: Progress Publishers, 1986), p. 830.
8. Karl Marx, *Das Kapital*, Erster Band (Berlin: Dietz Verlag, 1981), p. 85.
9. Ibid., n.
10. V.D. Savarkar, *Essentials of Hindutva* (1923).
11. Ibid.
12. See Etienne Balibar, *Politics and the Other Scene* ((London: Verso, 2005), p. X.
13. See Shamsul Islam, *Golwalkar's We or Our Nation Defined. A Critique with the Full Text of the Book* (New Delhi: Pharos Media, 2006), p. 14.
14. Novalis, 'Christianity or Europe. A Fragment', in *The Early Political Writings of the German Romantics*, ed. Frederick C. Beiser (Cambridge: Cambridge University Press, 1996), pp. 61-2.
15. Savitri Devi, *Warning to the Hindus* (Calcutta: Hindu Mission, 1939), p. 142. Also see my 'In Defence of Marxism', in *Critique*, Vol. 40, No. 1, February 2012.
16. Karl Marx and Frederick Engels, 'Manifesto of the Communist Party', in *Marx. Engels. Selected Works* (Moscow: Progress Publishers, 1977) p. 37.
17. Kancha Ilaiah, *Why I Am Not a Hindu. A Sudra Critique of Hindutva Philosophy, Culture and Political Economy* (Calcutta: Samya, 2003), p. XII.

18. Karl Marx, 'To L. Kugelmann in Hanover, London, April, 17, 1871', in *Marx. Engels. Selected Works* (Moscow: Progress Publishers, 1975), p. 671. See also Frederick Engels , 'Introduction to Karl Marx's *Civil War in France*' and Karl Marx, 'Civil War in France', in *Marx. Engels. Selected Works* (Moscow: Progress Publishers, 1975), pp. 258-9, 285, 289-90.
19. V.I. Lenin, 'The Dual Power', in *V.I. Lenin. Selected Works in Three Volumes*, Vol. 2 (Moscow: Progress Publishers, 1977), pp. 34-5.
20. Ibid.
21. V.I. Lenin, 'The Task of the Proletariat in the Present Revolution', in *V.I. Lenin. Selected Works in Three Volumes*, Vol. 2 (Moscow: Progress Publishers, 1977), p. 31.
22. V.I. Lenin, 'The Dual Power', in *V.I. Lenin. Selected Works in Three Volumes*, Vol. 2, p. 34.
23. See Frederick Engels, 'Letter to Bebel, London, March 18-25, 1875', in *Marx. Engels. Selected Works* (Moscow: Progress Publishers, 1975), p. 335.
24. See Slavoj Žižek, 'Talking to Fictions. People & Beyond (Ricardo Sanin interviews Slavoj Žižek)', in *Critical Legal Thinking*, July 2, 2009.
25. Slavoj Žižek, 'A Plea for Leninist Intolerance', in *Critical Inquiry*, Winter, 2002.
26. Antonio Negri, *Reflections on Empire*, trans. Ed Emery (Cambridge: Polity Press, 2003), p. 29. See also my *The New Militants* (Delhi: Aakar Books, 2014).
27. Javeed Alam, *Classes Trapped in Castes: Left's Ongoing Predicament in India* (Nagarjuna Nagar: Centre for Scientific Socialism, 2011).
28. Karl Marx, *Das Kapital*, Erster Band (Berlin: Dietz Verlag, 1981), p. 52.
29. See Karl Marx, 'These on Feuerbach', in *Marx. Engels. Selected Works* (Moscow: Progress Publishers, 1975).
30. Slavoj Žižek, *The Sublime Object of Ideology* (London: Verso, 1989), p. XIII.
31. Ibid.
32. Karl Marx, *Capital*, Vol. III, p. 558.

3

Hindutva, the Asiatic Mode of Production and the Indian Revolution

> Finally, in the struggle against the revolution, the parliamentary republic found itself compelled to strengthen, along with the repressive powers the resources and centralization of governmental power. All revolutions perfected this machine instead of smashing it. The parties that contended in turn for domination regarded the possession of this huge state edifice as the principal spoils of the victor.
>
> But under the absolute monarchy, during the first Revolution, under Napoleon, bureaucracy was only the means of preparing the class rule of the bourgeoisie. Under the Restoration, under Louis Philippe, under the parliamentary republic, it was the instrument of the ruling class, however much it strove for power of its own.
>
> *Karl Marx*

> A closer investigation of a man's day-dreams generally shows that all his heroic exploits are carried out and all his success achieved only in order to please a woman and to be preferred by her to other men. These phantasies are satisfactions of wishes proceeding from deprivation and longing.
>
> *Sigmund Freud*

Introduction

While the fundamentals of this chapter were drafted before the Indian Bonaparte, Narendra Modi, found that a phantasmagorical crown of eternal glory was put on his temporal head, where for the first time Indian fascism has won electoral victory in parliamentary elections with a clear majority; the terrible ghost of fascism that has become an even more terrible reality makes us ponder on the deeper structures of fascism in India. It thus explores the mass psychology of fascism in India. It also explores the historical materialist mechanisms of fascism's recent triumph in the 2014 National Elections. While it is known that the term "Hindutva" (coined by Savarkar in the 1920s when Mussolini was capturing power in Italy) is the basis for the political philosophy of Indian fascism, the deeper structures of caste-stratified Hinduism (as the religio-culture of pre-capitalist India) have not been explored at the scientific level such that a radical left movement can uproot this anti-humanist, anti-people's ideology of pre-capitalist India.

Besides ignoring the caste question as a structural component of the mode of production in India, as also ignoring the symptomatic fetish of caste-stratified society called "Hinduism", the greatest error of the Established Left was to become part of the parliamentary political order, forgetting that for Marx (a point which Lenin reminded us in *State and Revolution*), revolutionary politics emerges from *outside* the state order and against the state order. They forgot what Marx had once said that "the working class cannot simply lay hold of the ready-made state machinery, and wield it for its own purposes".[1] They forgot that "State power assumed...the character of the national power of capital over labour, of a public force organized for social enslavement, of an engine of class despotism".[2] Despite it being well known that the state with its magical representation that "soared high above society" was merely the "greatest scandal of that society" and the "very hotbed of all its corruptions";[3] the Established Left continued to be part of this magical and corrupt hotbed. The triumph of Modi is the triumph of the neo-liberal right-wing control of the hotbed of corruption. The left cannot be part of this hotbed;

and yet the Stalinist Established Left insists on being cosy there. They did not know that one day; the cosy bed of corruption would show its brutal face as the engine of class despotism and erupt as the triumph of fascism.

This chapter is on how the Revolutionary Left needs enacting the Revolution in ways entirely different that what the left in India had imagined. First, it will have to encounter caste within the matrix of the Asiatic mode of production, and then see modern classes emerging from this Asiatic mode, and finally fighting from outside the state mechanism. Its mobilization shall not traverse the paths of liberal democracy. Our type of Marxism shall neither be the type common to the liberals or the Legal Marxists. Marx's teachings are not the same as that of Peter Struve—the founder of "Legal Marxism".

Further, the Revolution is not an "Event" (even of the type that Alain Badiou talks of). Nor is it the one following the laws ordained by the Stalinists. Instead the Revolution is a type of process, which involves real people with real needs. Historicism and humanism are thus its cornerstones. And since one understands the Revolution as a real human event, the articulation of the cultural superstructure is of great importance.

There are two basic parts of this chapter: (1) of actively engaging the political and ideology superstructure of Indian fascism, and (2) of understanding the dynamics of caste-class hegemony (within the Indian variant of the Asiatic mode of production in the era of late imperialism in permanent crisis). Thus the logic of the decomposition of caste along with the neurotic recomposition of caste (from which emerges the mass psychology of Indian fascism) forms the logic of the rise of fascism in India. Two of B.R. Ambedkar's observations of caste are located as the basis for understanding the rise of fascism in India: (1) that it is a system of graded inequality, and (2) a system of not only division of labour, but a system of division of labourers. Along with these observations, we relate Marx's theories of alienation and the reification of society with caste-stratification and how caste-stratification becomes an Indian form of racism which finally culminates in Indian fascism.

On Freudo-Marxism as a Rational Science

We begin, however with a line from Ambedkar's *Annihilation of Caste* which is a type of remembrance that ought to provoke the rational mind to discuss the almost psychotic religio-cultural structure of pre-capitalist India. That Ambedkar's words: the "ideal Hindu" is "refusing to have contact with others" corresponds to Sigmund Freud's definition of psychosis as the "complete withdrawal from reality",[4] is a matter that must be stressed. And with the understanding of this psychotic withdrawal from reality, one turns to the understanding how fascism becomes popular with its racist idea of nationhood combined with its ideology of celebration of riots and wars. We are stressing this racist idea of nationhood, for both Savarkar's *Hindutva* and M.S. Golwalkar's *We or Our Nation Defined* talked of the "race spirit", implying an imagined "Hindu race" that was supposed to be in perpetual war with an even more imagined "Muslim race".

For Ambedkar it was most certain: Hinduism as the religio-culture of pre-capitalist India had to go, for any form of democracy to really survive and thrive in India. While the basis of this chapter is political in a Revolutionary Marxist sense (where the entire project of "Hindutva" is critiqued), the very fundamental point in this chapter is a materialist dialectical methodology that locates Hinduism as the religio-culture of pre-capitalist India—that despite the "Protestant reform" that it has undergone to create the spirit of liberal capitalism: to borrow from Max Weber's repertoire—has allowed Hindutva fascism to emerge victorious. This Hinduism as the symptomatic symptom of caste-stratified society turning to Hindutva fascism forms the groundwork of our analysis.

Freudo-Marxism deals specifically with ideology-critique and the historicist and humanist analysis of superstructures.

Unlike the Established Left that was bred on the Stalinist "reflection theory" which stated that the political and ideology superstructure was only a "reflection" or "copy" of the economic base, we deal with an entirely different way of looking at Marxism, especially in dealing with the mass psychology of fascism. Thus we transform the classical Marxist theorem: the economic base determines the political and ideological superstructure into a new model: *the reified-economic base of capitalism in permanent crisis determines the estranged-psychotic mind of fascism.*

What one needs to do is to create scientific tools to analyze fascism in India. Freud, here, enters the scientific scene of action. What one does is that one transforms his idea of "hysterical phantasies" in the arena of libidinal economy into the arena of political economy of the ideology of fascism. Consider Freud's own idea of phantasy. Consider how Narendra Modi projected as "SuperModi" by the Media Industry[5] is understood as the collective wish-phantasy produced by the Media Industry, but a wish-phantasy which is based however on economic scarcity and mental deprivation. Note the ideas of the "erotic and ambitious" nature in human beings in the passage below. Note what Freud calls "the delusional imaginations of the paranoiac, which are concerned with the greatness and the sufferings of his own self".[6] Try to relate this delusional imagination of the suffering character, with the character-image of the superman (Narendra Modi) constructed by the Media Industry. Note also this psychoanalytic presentation: "The strange performances with which certain perverts stage their sexual satisfaction".[7] Since we are relating the idea of the delusional imaginations of the paranoiac-pervert combine with the phantasmagorical images produced of the suffering hero by the Media Industry, we say (following Freud) that this psychical structure of the paranoid-turned-hero is present in all psychoneuroses particularly in hysterical phantasies.[8] Taking these and relating with the fascist personality as the heroic character portrayed by the Media Industry, we turn to the consideration of the following:

> A common source and normal prototype of all these *creations of phantasy* is to be found in what are called the *day dreams of youth*. These have already received some, though as yet insufficient, notice in the literature of the subject. They occur with perhaps equal frequency in both sexes, though it seems that while in girls and women they are invariably of an erotic nature, in men they may be *either erotic or ambitious*. Nevertheless the importance of the erotic factor in men, too, should not be given a secondary rating; a closer investigation of a man's day-dreams generally shows that *all his heroic exploits are carried out and all his success achieved only in order to please a woman and to be preferred by her to other men. These phantasies are satisfactions of wishes proceeding from deprivation and longing*. They are justly called 'day-dreams', for they give us the key to an understanding of night-dreams—in which the nucleus of the dream-formation consists of nothing else than complicated day-time phantasies of this kind that they have been distorted and are misunderstood by the conscious psychical agency (all emphasis mine. M.J.).[9]

What Revolutionary Marxism has to do, is relate this psychoanalytic understanding with special reference to "these phantasies of satisfactions of wishes proceeding from deprivation and longing". Once one understands this psychoanalytic political economy of deprivation, one will be able to understand why the masses consume the ideologies of the far-right. Thus if there is the mode of production of ideas, there is also the mode of consumption, mediated by the mode of distribution of these ideas. And that is why one insists that a *scientific theory of the mode of production of ideology is necessary*. What a scientific theory of the mode of production of ideology does is that it probes into the deep structures of the "unconscious phantasy".[10]

The tragedy is that, by and large, the Established Left in India from S.A. Dange to Prakash Karat bypassed this materialist analysis, to be deceived by forms of reasoning that have almost nothing to do with good Marxist scholarship, but had much to do with dubious and duplicate scholarship that grew from the cranium of the Stalinist counterrevolution in the Soviet Union since 1928. The complete drubbing of the Established Left in the 2014 National Elections is proof of their dubious scholarship. Reasons of their split from the masses are manifold: one reason being that they could not have a scientific theory of the mode of production of ideology. They could not understand how ideologies are produced and consumed. The other reason is that they could not understand Marx's original theory of historical materialism, especially his theory of *complex histories* and his critique of unilinear historicism.

Caste-Class Dialectic

And because they could not have these two ideas that Marx himself analyzed, this Established Left in India could not articulate class conjectures, especially the emergence of the modern proletariat from the decaying Indian village system. It thus could not articulate the caste-class dialectic. For the Established Left, caste and class are the two unfortunate souls that dwell in their Faustian breast. Besides the inability in understanding this caste-class dialectic, they could not understand in depth the lethal character of caste and Hinduism as the religio-culture of pre-capitalist India.

This chapter is consequently critical of the Established Left's deficit analysis of caste and surplus analysis of "Indian feudalism", an analysis that restricted caste only as a social system of an imagined 'feudal' India. Modern classes are almost inevitably tied down to the caste system—its decomposition and recomposition—and the Established Left has altogether forgotten this relation between modern classes and the caste system. This chapter, besides taking the ideologies of Hinduism and Hindutva as the mass psychology of fascism, will also be critical of the analysis of classes in contemporary India combined with the critique of the theory of transition of pre-capitalism to capitalism in India. This critique is constituted in Marx's original theory of the Asiatic mode of production which questions the very existence of feudalism in India. And because of the questioning of feudalism in India, this chapter also questions the methodological tools in understanding the transition of pre-capitalism to capitalism in India.

This lack of understanding the nature of pre-capitalist India, this lack of understanding caste in both Indian history and in the political economy of global capital accumulation, besides forgetting the consequent caste-class dialectic has led to the misunderstanding of the nature of contemporary popular classes, or what one may call the "basic classes" in India. These lacks have further led to the alienation of the Established Left from the popular classes. This *alienation* has led to a *vacuum* which is being filled by the Hindutva fascists. For it is this precise *alienated vacuum* that the fascists have mastered. *Fascism is the mastery and manipulation of alienation and alienated vacuums.*

And because concrete classes were replaced by abstract classes (according to the transcendental imagination of the Established Left), concrete history was replaced by abstract history. Duplicate classes and duplicate history marched onto the scene of Indian history. And that is why we are saying that the main critique is of the abstract-universal theory of history that is sacrosanct for the Established Left in India, a theory first propounded in modern times by Immanuel Kant (that laid the basis of the theory of history determined by iron laws independent of humanity) as well as the critique of the *general theory of history* that has its origins in Stalin's counterrevolution and manipulation of Marxism. Remember it was Stalin (since the early 1930s) who literally banned any debate on the Asiatic mode of production. The debate on the Asiatic mode of production was officially banned in the Soviet Union in 1931. In 1933 V.V. Struve's theory that the ancient east (like Western Europe) also had a slave owning mode of production was adopted. Though the Soviets after Stalin's death re-opened the debate in 1964 followed in France by the works of Maurice Godelier and Suret-Canale; in India the pattern of history writing was determined by R.S. Sharma's *Indian Feudalism* followed by the works of Irfan Habib that followed the Stalinist unilinear model. More recently it is Kevin Anderson who has challenged the Stalinist view by raising the importance of a more nuanced reading of Marx on non-Western societies in his *Marx at the Margins*.

Dialectical and Historical-Humanist Materialism

My contention is that one cannot locate the questions of caste, its relation to the modern class system and capital accumulation which has led to the triumph of Indian fascism when one operates with the fallacious question of understanding history as unilinear history—of history determined by so-called "iron laws". It must be noted that this view of history as the march-past of "iron laws" that run independent of humanity was part of the discourse of the Second International. The fact that it was then canonized by Stalin and then converted to gospel truth seems to be ignored by even the most serious social scientists studying caste. Recall that this misinterpretation of Marx was based on the theory of inevitability of historical 'happenings' based itself on the almost conscious ignorance of Marx's *Economic and Philosophic Manuscripts of 1844* and the *Ethnological Notebooks*. The fact that Marx almost never used the term *unvermeidliche* (or "inevitable") and that it was an almost unwitting inclusion by Engels seems totally forgotten by social science. Recall Marx's humanist understanding of history:

> *History* does *nothing*, it 'possesses no immense wealth', it 'wages *no* battles'. It is the *human*, real, living humanity who does all that, who possess all that; 'history', is not, as it were, a person apart, using humanity as a means to achieve *its own* aims; history is *nothing but* human activity pursuing its aims.[11]

It is in this epistemic space that we claim that the classical understanding of Marxism as dialectical and humanist materialist needs to be re-thought as dialectical and historical-humanist materialism. It is in this very space that one locates the positivist understanding of history that Indian Marxists of the most serious calibre from Kosambi to R.S. Sharma and Irfan Habib fell prey to. The fact that Marx's *Economic and Philosophic Manuscripts of 1844* and the *Ethnological Notebooks* are absent from their theoretical repertoire needs being stressed. The fact that even Gramsci and Lukács are absent not to forget Raya Dunayevskaya needs also to be re-stressed. What one needs to do is link Marxism as historicism and humanism with the idea of multilinear historicism.

We have already noted that this idea of *multilinear historicism* which Marx had introduced in the lexicon of historical materialism lies largely forgotten. Soviet historians like S. Shmonin who advocated the idea of the Asiatic mode in 1929 were never referred to in either Marxist discussions on history or in radical politics, nor was Plekhanov's *History of Russian Social Thought* (where the Asiatic mode was located) taken seriously. By 1931 there were no references to this mode in discussions in the Soviet Union. Not only was the discussion under Stalin purged—M.D. Kokin, the Soviet proponent of this idea, died in the Stalinist anti-communist genocide—but even Marxist scholars like G.A. Cohen, Maurice Dobb and Paul Sweezy made no reference to it. Likewise Edward Said thought that the Asiatic mode of production was an Orientalist intervention and Marx became a Romantic and Messianic Orientalist, condemning non-European societies to eternal backwardness.[12]

Repercussions of this theme of ignoring the Asiatic mode of production is that history was made to look like the infamous march-past of iron laws. According to this thesis, capitalism could only emerge from feudalism, while communism could only grow from capitalism. And since India is not capitalist (or not "fully developed" capitalist), communism would have to wait like the missing messiah. That there are views (Kevin

Anderson is an example) that capitalism emerged in India not from feudalism, but from a complex origin determined in the last resort by the dissolution of the village communities and the primitive commune property system[13] is also an idea that is largely not known. It is the Indian Maoist (albeit unwittingly) who has taken the view of tribal commune property—the *ager publicus* (public lands) of Marx's *pre-capitalist economic formations*—as the pivotal force for the Indian revolution. However since they do not locate this thesis in the larger genre of the Asiatic mode of production, their old thesis of semi-feudalism and the New Democratic Revolution are reified as the rocks to which Indian Prometheus is permanently chained. Neither the parliamentary left nor the Maoists have ever thought that communism in India can come directly by simply skipping over capitalism. And this inability of thinking how to skip the entire capitalist mode of production has led to a vacuum from where fascism has emerged.

In this perspective of multilinear historicism one recalls Marx's phrase that just as the history of the expropriation of the peasantry "in different countries, assumes different aspects", so too the emergence of the modern proletariat takes different forms.[14] And since it was only in England that took what Marx calls the "classical form"[15], one cannot remain enslaved to this European form of capitalism. *Nor does one, as Marx insists, pass through the dreadful vicissitudes of capitalism.*[16]

That the articulation of the parliamentary left who want to march with the myth of historical inevitabilities is in direct opposition to Marx's formulation of *jumps in history* determined by the radical politics of permanent revolution, also ought to be noted. They seem to have forgotten that the "historical inevitability" of the rise of capitalism that involves the divorcing of the producer from the means of production was limited only to Western Europe.[17] One cannot impose this history onto the entire world. As Marx said with regard to another Narodniki, Mikhailovsky, there is no "general path of development prescribed by fate to all nations" where one could impose a "general historico-philosophical theory" onto the entire world.[18] Recall Marx again "the supreme virtue of this (understanding) consists in being supra-historical."[19]

Keeping this very important theme of multilinearism in mind, one is able to locate the complexity of Indian history. One is also able to see how Indian history keeps its pre-capitalist formations within its capitalist breast and thus hops on its two feet—one being the archaic caste foot, the other the modern class foot. And because the caste foot is ahead of the class foot one can say that, "one suffers not only from the development of capitalist production, but also from the incompleteness of that development."[20] The tragedy of Indian history is that it shall be haunted not merely by the incompleteness of bourgeois development, but by the impossibility of this alleged "full development". It is in the womb of this underdevelopment that one reads Marx's viewing of the Oriental state as the *despotic sovereign*, along with the village communities that are said to be "contaminated by caste and slavery".[21] At one level the caste system seems to echo Marx's views of feudal Europe stuck with its idiocy and superstition. At another level it is concrete and anticipates Ambedkar's critique of the caste system where caste not only degrades and saps the energies of the peasants and the menial castes, but degrades humanity as a whole.

But besides these two very well known formations, Marx also talks of the communes that are said to have vitality that are superior not only to Greek and Roman societies, but also compared to modern societies.[22] The communes thus had to be preserved.[23] Not only were these communes to be preserved, they were to be the springboard for direct communist revolutions. One thus distinguishes the spaces of *Gemeinschaft* (community) and *Gemeinwesen* (commune) within the space of pre-capitalist societies. Pre-capitalism is not one single, undifferentiated space. It most certainly is not destined to go through capitalism. One could jump directly from this

Gemeinwesen (commune) to modern communism, while the site of the caste-based *Gemeinschaft* was fit only to be destroyed lock, stock and barrel.

To claim that the communes were to die out due to the necessity of some inexorable law of history (rather: Law of History) was for Marx an outrageous imperialist lie. Let us put Marx's commune at the background and re-think tribal India and the struggles being carried there. One must note how the Indian state has declared these struggles—i.e. struggles against the corporate colonization of the Indian forests—as terrorism of the highest order. Consider then Marx as how to theorize in this space of combined and uneven development and how the communes could be preserved:

> One should be on one's guard when reading the histories of primitive communities written by bourgeois historians. They do not stop at anything, even outright distortion. Sir Henry Maine, for example, who was an ardent active supporter of the British government in its policy of destroying Indian communes by force, tells us hypocritically that all noble efforts on the part of the government to support these communes were thwarted by the elementary force of these laws![24]

A small note on this writing of history by the Indian left who have totally forgotten Marx's original contribution is thus necessary. Irfan Habib, for instance, while theorizing on the Marxist understanding of Indian history mentions solely the 1959 and 1976 Moscow editions of Marx on India,[25] alongside selected correspondence between Marx and Engels. The complex arguments of Marx on pre-capitalist societies are almost left untouched. Marx's *Ethnological Notebooks*, first published in 1974, which include Marx's notes on Morgan, Phear, Maine, Lubbock and Kovalevsky, are not even vaguely referred to by Habib. They are, so Habib claims, "not available to me".[26] Since Habib (and one should say all those who subscribe to the erroneous theory of "Indian feudalism") does not take the extreme complex dialectic of the communes, village communities and the authoritarian Asiatic state as a dialectic of combined and uneven social formation, he reduces Marx to a thinker, who like the Orientalists before him, theorized on an "unchanging" East, calling Marx's formulation extremely "unjust" and "highly idealized",[27] sometimes also appearing as a fellow traveller of not only Hegel, but also Macaulay.[28] Marx was said to have a "mystical view of property"[29] and he also worked with "inherited generalizations",[30] usually borrowed from the Eurocentric baggage of Hegelian metaphysics. One must however note that Habib is one of the most important Marxist historians and his reading has to be taken very seriously. Our response is that Marx's dynamics of non-capitalist societies was not taken seriously enough to gauge the nature of the revolutionary forces inherent in Indian history.

Once this mode of theorization is understood one is able to move into the readings of the question of caste in the contexts of the modes of production debate, with special emphasis on understanding non-European history. One thus re-emphasizes how the question of the readings of the *Grundrisse*, Marx's letter to Vera Zasulich and the *Ethnological Notebooks* can be kept in its scientific perspective. The caste question is analyzed from this perspective of multi-linear historicism. One also analyzes caste from the perspective of ideology critique and state power in India.

Now it is well known that Indian Marxism by and large shares an ambivalent relation to the caste question. This ambivalent character seems to stem from the fact that Marx's views on the non-capitalist Western world was ignored whereby the history of Western Europe (especially the question of the transition of feudalism to capitalism in Europe) was imposed as a readymade model to be imposed on *all* societies. This fallacy has been disastrous for not only the Indian revolution, but also for Indian democracy, as the subject of both revolution and democracy could not be found. To talk of the industrial proletariat as the revolutionary subject independent of the concrete history of South Asia (as theorized by the mainstream parliamentary left), or to talk of the peasants as the subject of Indian history (as the Maoists do), are abstract questions posed, questions which are independent of the real history of South Asia, thus independent of the history of social structures that comprise of castes (and if not non-capitalist communities then at least pre-capitalist communities). The parliamentary left with their abstract theory of Indian history would turn to a form of social engineering that is totally alien to the spirit of science.

We thus re-emphasize the articulation of caste in India and the imperative to theorize on this peculiar phenomenon from a non-essentialist historical materialist problematic. In this sense it is in contrast to thinkers in the genre of not only the Stalinists, not only in contrast to the problematic of Edward Said and his postmodern followers, but primarily in contrast to the giants of contemporary social science, namely, Louis Dumont and Nicholas Dirks. While the former seemed to essentialize caste—Habib calls his theory the "Western sociologist's image of the caste system"[31]—the latter understands caste as a modern phenomenon not belonging to pre-colonial India, but as an Orientalist fantasy and colonial construct to manage and govern the Eastern frontiers of the British Empire, even a form of what he calls a "peculiar form of modern Western nostalgia."[32] In this Dirksean sense an Orientalist reading of caste as the "central symbol" of Indian civilization[33] entirely misses the point both of the colonial narrative and the political economy of imperialism. If it were the British that reified caste, as Dirks suggests[34], then the reading of caste had to change, a change that would directly challenge not only the understanding of caste from Marx and Weber to Dumont, but also challenge Ambedkar's radical thesis.[35] Dirks' epistemic repertoire is, as must be pointed out, borrowed from Michel Foucault and Edward Said. That Dirks is silent on Foucault's seeming contempt of the power/knowledge nexus of so-called "Western civilization" and his fascination for Asian fascists like Ayatollah

Khomeini must also be noted. In this space one raises the question: "If caste is merely a colonial invention devoid of its pre-capitalist genealogy, then would not the Dirks inspired thesis also fall in the same trap that Foucault fell into, namely of supporting Ayatollah Khomeini and Asian fascism?"

Debating the Caste Question

Let us situate this question in contemporary debates and move from the posing of these questions to a recent question that has been posed by Prabhat Patnaik which he calls "the decline of left", a question that he answers as a form an empiricization where the left have not been able to champion the cause of the transcendence of capitalism. Though what is surprising is that Patnaik does not anywhere in this essay mention caste, one must note that somewhere earlier he does mention the question of caste as a central problem in Indian history and politics when referring to E.M.S. Namboodiripad.[36]

I shall take this question posed by Patnaik to understand how caste has to be understood as a silent counterrevolution. Now what caste as the silent counterrevolution did was relegate the Indian labour force—the artisans and the craftspeople, the Shudras and the ati-Shudras) as the hellish other and the unclean untouchables. But what this counterrevolution also did was that it relegated the material practices of the Indian subaltern castes-classes and their ideologies of these material practices within the lowest order of things. The other side of the counter-revolution led to the privileging of the so-called 'spiritualizing' character of the Brahman overlords, a 'spiritualizing' that went from Adi Shankar and Manu to the Arya Samjis and Gandhianism that culminated on the one hand in the conservative character of India's liberalism and on the other hand to the formation of the Indian communal-fascists. The triumph of idealism over popular materialism led to the triumph of the Brahmans, a triumph that unfortunately yet stays with us.

What I would like to state is that in privileging its so-called spiritualization and its hierarchical system, Brahmanical overlordship also institutionalized stagnation and thus introduced an Indian form of Confucianism. Most importantly what it did was create an institution of graded inequality that prevented revolt by the subaltern castes-classes. Since we are using the term "caste-class" we shall raise the important question: "what is caste?" So what is caste, at least for Marx whose critique of Indian dominant class structure, comprised of this caste-class system, and was not to be seen as a West European version of class as the Indian left has championed? For Marx, castes, as ossified and frozen classes determined by the totem of purity and anti-humanism and the taboo of intersubjectivity, are social groups "separated from one another, without the right of intermarriage, with quite different status; each with its exclusive, unchangeable occupation".[37]

And yet the question of caste as race seems to elude this definition if caste is taken only at the level of economism and viewed as mere forms of pre-capitalist social communities. What one can argue (following Phule) is that the logic of caste follows the cultural and political logic of race, or (following Ambedkar) that caste emerged with the counterrevolution against Buddhism (it is exploitation and anti-humanism, but not the European version of racism), or (as now articulated by Nicholas Dirks) that it is of very late dating, 1857 to be precise, when the British sought to administer India in a "new" way. According to this thesis of Dirks, the British started extensive ethnographical studies to ethnicize caste. The census was used as a sociological tool to administer society on ethnic lines, since the 1871 census, followed by the 1881 one.[38] The issue for Dirks is how caste was able to "exercise such pride of place in the colonial imagination."[39] Caste is an "invention", a colonial one, or even worse, a modern one[40]. There are two themes that follow: one that caste has not been a trans-historical essence of Indian civilization, "an unchanged survival of ancient India", but the product of the encounter of India with colonial Britain.[41] In this case, caste, as we know it, ought not to be confused as the core of Indian civilization.

Contrary to Dirks, one will state that the underlying structure of Indian society is a complex structure of *caste-class*. Though thinkers did not view it as race (Max Weber, besides Aṃbedkar, was one of those thinkers), one will have to state that as *varna* in Sanskrit, caste implies "colour". The racial reference is obvious from its etymology, while the class implications follow. One is left with a dilemma: caste is not race, but is an Asian form of racism. The caste system cannot be merely seen as a social division of labour without seeing the question of racism, and the racial lines of hierarchy, segregation and exploitation. But then I have also followed the Indian Fanonists (i.e. the Frantz Fanon type of revolutionary politics, particularly Phule) in also identifying caste not only based on an Asian form of race-based domination, but also as we keep on insisting as a system of neurosis and psychosis, that gives birth to the cultural and political logic of counterrevolution in India and Indian fascism.

One will have to relocate this debate of caste as a form of racism and also try to understand this intellectual history. For us casteism is racism, and caste structured as an Indian form of race classification. Remember that Ambedkar did not want to give any space to the Brahmans to argue out their form of imagined superiority, by giving them the status of descendants from a European race. One should re-read his *Annihilation of Caste*, *Castes in India* and *Who Were the Shudras?* in light of the Asiatic mode of production to re-think the question of casteism as racism. The Brahmans are, as we all very well know, tricky customers. For if one brings in the "race question" (of the European variety) the Brahmans would only be too happy to claim affinity with the bourgeois Europeans. Thus the Brahmans were only too happy to accept this colonial race theory to justify the Indian mode of exploitation. Therefore Ambedkar's quote from *Annihilation of Caste* "the caste system does not demarcate racial division"[42] will have to be seen in a different light from those of mainstream European sociology. For Ambedkar Hinduism is essentially anti-humanist.[43]

Views on caste as race are diverse. Phule built his model of the Dalit-Bahujan (the Indian subalterns) on the presumption that the upper caste Brahmans were of Iranian (Aryan) origin who conquered an indigenous tribal people. I do feel that it is necessary to mobilize this narrative to encounter the unhappy consciousness of caste psychosis. For Phule, British colonialism was a form of modern colonialism. The real colonialism, which I call the *Ur-colonialism,* stems from the invasion of the Iranian tribes on the Indo-Gangetic plains. Hinduism is actually Brahmanism (or Aryanism) and the colonialism of the Indian life-world. One also needs to stress that evidence of the invasion of the Rg Vedic Iranian tribesmen can be found in the *Rg Veda* (the first text and consequently master text of 'Hinduism').[44] Evidence of the clash between the Avestan Iranians and the Rg Vedic tribes can also be found in the Iranian *Avesta,* the Collected Works of the Zoroastrians. For Phule, the upper castes cannot be considered as nationalists. Indian nationalism has to be built on different grounds—on not only non-Brahmanical, but primarily on non-Hindu grounds. Phule's thesis is most radical and has to be mobilized by the radical left in India. Here I will differ with Romila Thapar who claims that Phule was influenced by Orientalism (especially by the "Aryan question").[45] One must note that the word, "Aryan" in Indo-Iranian literature—that of the Rg Vedic people, the Zoroastrians and the Buddhists—is primarily said to be of linguist usage. It is said not to be a racial and racist issue. Yet things can always get complicated. While the pre-Islamic Iranians called their homeland *"Airyana Vaeja"* (or the "Aryan Expanse") which later became *Iran-Vej* and now Iran, the spectre of fascism can always hover around. The contemporary hatred of the Iranian regime towards Israel is not that it dislikes imperialism, but the Jews who are considered the "other" of the Aryans. Likewise for the Indian fascist organization, the RSS that built its ideology on the grounds of the fictitious "Aryan-Hindu" as the superior race, that conflicts with the imaginary "Semitic Muslims".

What we have done is equated caste with race and also claimed that since caste is understood as inherited class status that also has endogamy and the ideas of purity and pollution in its ideological cranium, then we have also claimed that this very brazen and subtle form of exclusion has necessarily to be understood as a problem of racism. In this sense Marx's idea of relations of production have turned into Ambedkar's idea of graded inequality, such that the analysis of classes in India does not merely have to concentrate on the type of surplus extraction, but have to analyze this surplus extraction in the structure of graded inequality.

Now graded inequality becomes not only the base of Indian relations of production, but also the base of the Indian counterrevolution. For the Indian notion of graded inequality was and is different from the European one (whether slave, feudal or capitalist), in the sense that in the European one the exploiter and exploited stand face to face. While it is true that European feudalism had "a complicated arrangement of society into various orders, a manifold gradation of social rank",[46] in the Indian type of inequality this complication would take an order similar to the one faced by the neurotic and the psychotic such that recognition of the exploiter and the class enemy becomes difficult, if not altogether impossible.

Keeping these points in mind, we recall the apt and rather chilling metaphor borrowed from Lenin: "None of the (Indian, my insertion, M.J.) Marxists understood Marx".[47] And what for Lenin have the Marxists who have not understood Marx not understood in Marx? They have not understood the question of dialectics. They have thus not understood multilinear historicism and thus not understood the algebra of the revolution. They have not understood the logic of insurrection and thus not understood how insurrection becomes an art form. They have not understood it because their psychotic Brahman head detached from the rest of the Shudra body does not allow it.

Thinking of Insurrection as Art

It is thus, that one understands how the Indian Marxists, dominated by their legal and ideological fetishes, have not been able to understand dialectics and insurrection as art. They have not understood it because it because they do not want insurrection, because they want the bourgeois status quo and because like Shakespeare's Cassius (from *Julius Caesar*) they not only think too much, but because they have monopolized all thinking. They thus become dangerous. Like Cassius they think, in fact think too much, think in terms of surplus thinking, thinking like surplus value, thinking that involves unpaid labour, thinking that does not merely mime the Kautskyite-Stalinist cliché "the proletariat cannot think in terms of revolution, the petty bourgeois does that", thus not allowing anyone else to think, nor act. Surplus thinking as non-thinking is necessarily anti-praxis. It is the sign of the Indian counterrevolution that not only devoured the Indian liberals, but also the left.

And that is why one insists on theorizing on Marx's original idea of the Asiatic mode of production with caste forming the nucleus for the understanding of social formations in India. By transforming the Marxist dictum: *the economic base determines the political and ideological superstructure* into *the reified base determines the unhappy consciousness and the estranged caste-based mind,* a Marxist imagination of radical historization transforms the nature of Indian politics. And that is why we say that the Indian left's deficit analysis of caste and surplus analysis of "Indian feudalism" has led to the catastrophic understanding of the analysis of classes in contemporary India. It has also misunderstood the theory of transition of pre-capitalism to capitalism in India. One has to be critical of this bizarre 'general' theory of history that has its origins in Stalin's counterrevolution and manipulation of Marxism. Meanwhile the necessary Dalitization of Marxism is based on the above understanding where Marx's idea of communism as humanism and naturalism combined with Lenin's praxis of insurrection puts an end to caste and bourgeois class consciousness. In this sense we argue for a larger philosophical canvas for Revolutionary Marxism where Marx's critique of alienation is directly related to the Buddhist idea of *Dukha*. Remember for Marx the fundamental revolution is the transformation of the state of human alienation, just as for Ambedkar one had to radically transform the state of *Dukha*.

Once one locates this humanist revolution we are able to turn from Lenin's lamentation of the Marxists who cannot understand Marx to the Bolshevik thinker Carl Einstein's theory of "absolute art" that breaks the reified world. What we now do is that we transform this idea of absolute art into the politics of permanent revolution. Permanent revolution argues for the transformation of alienation-*Dukha*. What this permanent revolution does is break the hegemony of reality that appears in what Marx calls in the dual forms of reified object form and contemplation.[48] For contemplation is always in thrall of alienation-*Dukha*. The permanent revolution breaks the hegemony of this reification. It talks of *human sensuous activity*, or *praxis* itself.[49] Armed with this permanent revolution it also breaks free from the scholasticism of not only Brahmanism, but scholasticism in general.[50]

Our Indian left is in contrast to the celebrator of the permanent revolution. He works not only with the alienated and schizophrenic mechanisms of civil society and the state but also with the entire caste-class apparatus. He is not only the empiricist that Patnaik recently critiqued. He is the "stubborn empiric" as Trotsky described Stalin, the neurotic Oriental despot who has returned once again. And like the Slavic form of Stalinism, the Indian Stalinists have totally forgotten the problematic of alienation-*Dukha.* Their political discourses are consequently etched in permanent decline. The Stalinists work with the brutal distortion of facts. We recall Lukács' debunking of what these so-called "facts" (of bourgeoisdom), facts that are constituted in the abyss between thought and reality. "Facts" in this Lukácsian sense does not refer to real facts. Facts do not deal with reality but its exact opposite: *the distortion of reality.* This is so because the idea of dialectical totality eludes the regime of facts. This is what happens to the caste-class question when we have a complete distortion of facts coupled with the forgetfulness of the Asiatic mode of production:

> During the recent years, caste mobilization has become an important factor in shaping Indian politics. Ever since the issue of Mandal Commission reservations in government jobs for the OBCs came to the national agenda in 1989, it has left an impact on the evolution of national politics. For a Marxist and a Communist, it is not only necessary to assess this growing role of caste assertion in Indian political life but also to map out the manner in which the unity of the toilers is strengthened in order to achieve the People's Democratic Revolution. Unless, as PS (P. Sundaraya) always used to teach us, we tackle with clarity this important phenomenon, we will not be able to overcome the potentially disruptive role that caste mobilization can have on toilers' unity. It is for these reasons that this issue needs to be address with all seriousness.[51]

Another manner of looking at the caste-class question is more critical:

> However, the weakness of the democratic movement in India lies in the fact that struggles against caste oppression have not been carried out integrating the same with the struggles against class exploitation. These struggles have rather been conducted in isolation from each other. Struggles against the caste oppression which have ignored the class outlook have failed to make much dent against the caste system. At the same time, working class struggles conducted without any clear perspective against caste oppression—which erodes the unity of the working class—have

> failed to make big advances. Is it possible to build the unity of the working class without waging struggles against caste oppression and untouchability? This is a vital question thrown before the working class movement. The need of the hour is to simultaneously organize struggles against caste oppression and class exploitation and build mutual ties and links between those struggles.[52]

On the Dialectics of Action

It must be pointed out that Revolutionary Marxism is not reactive like the political practice of our contemporary parliamentary comrades. It does not let the upper caste-class elites (now joined by the Industrial Reserve Army of the OBCs) in the form of the fascists create mass hysteria, let them mobilize on communal grounds, let them break mosques followed by a pogrom and then by a genocide. It does not peacefully protest by passing a memorandum condemning the barbaric fascists. It actively confronts the fascists. It differentiates the *active Leninist force* from the *reactive Stalinist force*. It consequently *sets* the agenda for politics in India. Its philosophy is the *negation of negation*. It thus proclaims what Marx calls the "*dissolution of the hitherto existing world order*" by stating "the *secret of its own existence* (which is) the dissolution of that world order."[53]

Just as Marx once said: "Philosophy cannot be made a reality without the abolition of the proletariat, the proletariat cannot be abolished without philosophy being made a reality";[54] one now says this Marxist philosophy of humanity as humanity can be made a reality only with the abolition of the entire Indian mode of production with caste understood as class-clan-psychosis as the seed from which the terrible tree of Indian fascism has grown. But to accomplish this philosophy of humanity as humanity, India will have to witness and activate a revolution that uproots not only the tree of fascism that has grown from the seed of caste understood as class-clan-psychosis; but also have to uproot the other counterrevolutionary weeds—from the liberals, Stalinists and other neo-cons who are actively sabotaging the Indian Revolution. But for this to happen, one will have to discard the Old Comrades and search for New Militants. These New Militants do not want to be part of the state apparatus, but want to *smash the state*[55], along with the smashing of the capitalist economy itself.

But then, are the present comrades ready for this?

REFERENCES

1. Karl Marx, 'The Civil War in France', in *Marx. Engels. Selected Works* (Moscow: Progress Publishers, 1975), p. 285.
2. Ibid.
3. Ibid., p. 287.
4. B.R. Ambedkar, 'Annhilation of Caste', in *The Essential Writings of B.R. Ambedkar*, ed. Valerian Rodrigues (Delhi: Oxford University Press, 2008), p. 267. Also see Sigmund Freud, 'Neurosis and Psychosis', and 'The Loss of Reality in Neurosis and Psychosis', in *The Penguin Freud Library. Vol. 10. On Psychopathology* (London: Penguin, 1993), pp. 209-26.
5. *The Times of India*, May 17, 2014.
6. 'Hysterical Phantasies and Their Relation to Bisexuality', in *The Penguin Freud Library. Vol. 10. On Psychopathology* (London: Penguin, 1993), p. 87.
7. Ibid.
8. Ibid., p. 87.
9. Ibid., pp. 87-8.
10. Ibid., p. 88.
11. Karl Marx and Frederick Engels, *The Holy Family* (Moscow: Progress Publishers, 1980), p. 116. See also my *The Seductions of Karl Marx*, Delhi: Aakar Books, 2010, p. 71.
12. Edward Said, *Orientalism* (London: Penguin, 1978), pp. 154, 206.
13. Kevin Anderson, 'Marx's Late Writings on Russia Re-examined', in *News & Letters*, November (2007).
14. Karl Marx, 'First Draft of the Reply to V.I. Zasulich's Letter', in *Marx. Engels. Selected Works*, Vol. 3 (Moscow: Progress Publishers, 1970), p. 152.

15. Ibid.
16. Ibid., p. 153.
17. Ibid., p. 152.
18. Karl Marx, 'Letter to the Editorial Board of *Otechestvenniye Zapiski*, London, November, 1877', in *Marx. Engels. Selected Correspondence* (Moscow: Progress Publishers, (1975), p. 293.
19. Ibid., p. 294.
20. Karl Marx, *Capital*, Vol. I, p. 20.
21. Karl Marx, 'The British Rule in India', in *On Colonialism* (Moscow: Progress Publishers, 1976), p. 40.
22. Karl Marx, 'First Draft of the Reply to V.I. Zasulich's Letter', p. 154.
23. Ibid., p. 153.
24. Ibid., p. 154.
25. Irfan Habib, *Essays in Indian History. Towards a Marxist Perception* (New Delhi: Tulika Books, 1995), p. 14; and 'Marx's Perception of India', in Iqbal Husain, edited *Karl Marx. On India* (New Delhi: Tulika Books, 2006), p. XVIX.
26. Irfan Habib, 'Marx's Perception of India', p. XXXIV, n. 84.
27. Irfan Habib, *Essays in Indian History. Towards a Marxist Perception*, pp. 35, 234.
28. Irfan Habib, 'Marx's Perception of India', p. XXVII, n. 46.
29. Ibid., XXVI.
30. Ibid., XX-XXII.
31. Irfan Habib, 'Caste in Indian History', in *Essays in Indian History. Towards a Marxist Perception*, p. 164.
32. Nicholas Dirks, *Castes of Mind. Colonialism and the Makings of Modern India* (New Jersey: Princeton University Press, 2001), p. 5.
33. Ibid., pp. 3-4.
34. Ibid., p. 7.
35. But then it would also challenge the readings of Megasthenes and Alberuni and surprisingly put them too in the cultural baggage of Orientalism.
36. Prabhat Patnaik, 'E.M.S. Namoodiripad's Perception of History', in *The Marxist*, Vol. XXV, 3-4, July September, 2009.
37. Karl Marx, *Pre-Capitalist Economic Formations*, trans. Jack Cohen, edited with an introduction by E.J. Hobsbawm (London: Lawrence & Wishart, 1964), pp. 76-7.

38. Nicholas Dirks, *Castes of Mind. Colonialism and the Makings of Modern India.*
39. Ibid.
40. Ibid., pp. 3-18.
41. Ibid., p. 5.
42. See 'Annihilation of Caste', in *The Essential Writings of B.R. Ambedkar*, p. 265.
43. Ibid., p. 273.
44. See *Sacred Writings. Hinduism. Rg Veda*, trans. Ralf T.F. Griffith (New York: Quality Paperback Books, 1992), pp. 36, 397, 637, 638, 641, 642.
45. See Romila Thapar, *The Aryan. Recasting Constructs* (Gurgaon: Three Essays Collective, 2008).
46 Karl Marx and Fredrick Engels, 'Manifesto of the Communist Party', in *Marx. Engels. Selected Works* (Moscow: Progress Publishers, 1975), p. 36.
47. V.I. Lenin, *Philosophical Notebooks. Collected Works*, Vol. 38. (Moscow: Progress Publishers, 1980), p. 180.
48. Karl Marx, 'Theses on Feuerbach', in *Marx. Engels. Selected Works* (Moscow: Progress Publishers, 1975), p. 28.
49. Ibid.
50. Ibid.
51. Sitaram Yechury, 'Caste and Class in Indian Politics Today' (P. Sundaraya Memorial Lecture, 1997).
52. P. Sampath, 'Experiencing of Struggles against Untouchability in Tamil Nadu', in *The Marxist*, XXX, 1, January-March 2010.
53. Karl Marx, 'A Contribution to the Critique of Hegel's Philosophy of Right', in *Karl Marx. Early Writings*, trans. Rodney Livingstone and Gregor Benton (New York: Vintage Books, 1975), p. 256.
54. Ibid., p. 257.
55. The theme of the smashing of the state is central to Marx from *The Eighteenth Brumaire of Louis Bonaparte* to *The Civil War in France*. In the 1871 letter to Kugelmann, Marx talked of this *smashing of the state*, a theme that the Established Left in India has totally forgotten. See Marx, 'To Kugelmann, 1871', in *Marx. Engels. Selected Works* (Moscow: Progress Publishers, 1975), p. 670.

4
Why We Are Not Hindus: A Reply to the Indian Fascists

> The true picture of the past flits by. The past can be seized only as an image that flashes up at the instant when it can be recognized and is never seen again.
>
> *Walter Benjamin*

> However it is impossible to arrive at a workers' state with empty hands. Only political invalids can speak of a peaceful, constitutional road to socialism. The constitutional road is cut by trenches held by the fascist bands. There are not a few trenches before us. The bourgeois will not hesitate to resort to a dozen coup d'état, aided by the police and the army, to prevent the proletariat from coming to power.
>
> *Leon Trotsky*

Fascism and the Manipulation of Memory

With the global capitalist economy in depression that is leading the accumulation of capital to the accumulation of weapons and wars, and also with the victory of the Indian fascists in the 2014 National Elections, one has two open choices for humanity that Rosa Luxemburg had talked of a century before: socialism or barbarism. In India the two choices are—radical secularism or Hindutva. And yet it seems that neither the democratic parties, nor the Established Left led by the Communist Party of India (Marxist)—the CPI(M)—is taking this threat of fascist takeover in the times of economic crisis seriously. And in case if one is lost in liberal democratic and Stalinist slumbers in imagining that the fascist neo-cons are part of the democratic space, one only needs to remind them what the truth of Indian fascism is.

While the need of the hour is to understand the fascist pattern of propaganda and the ability to create mass hysteria which takes on a form of politics that is devoid of political thought, it is not the point of Revolutionary Marxism to take the path of parliamentary democracy to solve the problems of democracy and fascism. In a certain view-point we would agree with Alain Badiou and Žižek in stating that one should not be enamoured by the word "democracy", neither be scared by the word "totalitarianism". It must be said that the revolutionary understanding of democracy (the one argued by Lenin in *State and Revolution*) is totally different from what we know as "democracy". It must also be said that the social democratic understanding of democracy practised by the Indian Established Left, especially by the CPI(M) derives from the theoretical problematic inherited from Karl Kautsky's *The Dictatorship of the Proletariat*.

This chapter is a critique of the hegemonic discourses on fascism dominated by theories of economism and liberalism, which largely have ignored the philosophies of Phule and Ambedkar. Economism in India (as found in the politics of the Parliamentary Left) claims that the problem lies solely in a reductive interpretation of the economy, where fascism is said to be a "copy" or "reflection" of the hidden economic base; while liberalism says that the problem of fascism lies in intolerance and has nothing to do with political economy and the way the ruling classes manipulate religion. Consequently this chapter calls for a deeper Cultural Revolution that can displace fascist hegemony. Our critique is of the politics of "Hindutva"—the Sanskritized and Brahmanical tradition that the RSS has modelled after European fascism and the Westphalian idea of the nation state. Unlike the mainstream understanding that differentiates "Hindutva" from Hinduism proper—the first is said to be fascist while the latter is said to be a matter of faith and thus democratic—we follow the radical Ambedkarite line that critiques Hinduism itself as a Sanskritized and Brahmanical elitism and as a system that is inherently undemocratic. Like Marx said, "the critique of religion is the prerequisite of all criticism",[1] we say the critique of Hinduism is the basis of the critique of what one calls after Perry Anderson as the "Indian ideology". Hinduism, as one should note, is basically a concealed form of Brahmanism. While there have been attempts to construct a Brahman-free Hinduism, a form of Hinduism devoid of Brahmanism, I shall be following the Ambedkar line, namely that Hinduism is the cultural and intellectual matrix of Brahmanism, and that caste-stratification, anti-humanism and the regression of thinking are its essential principles.

We begin with this pertinent question: "What is the nature of Indian fascism?" We claim that it is based on a spurious idea of communitarianism, or estranged communitarianism where neither equality nor liberty exists. Here the national popular unity is disrupted for a fascist idea of the "people". One knows that this idea of the "people" (*Volk*) was the essence of German fascism based on the ideology of blood descent where the idea of citizenship was displaced for an idea of "community".

We know that for all fascists the question of Constitutional Democracy is not something to be hailed, but the "Hindu Rashtra", a mythical nation modelled after the Nazi idea of nationalism, where there would be no place for religious and ethnic minorities. In a certain sense it is not only Savarkar, K.B. Hedgewar and Golwalkar who are the constructors of this myth of the "Hindu nation", but also the Indian liberals, the main edifice that they inherited from Orientalism and colonialism. We know of course that it was Savarkar who first laid the political foundations of this theme, later to be taken by the RSS and made infamous by Golwalkar. That this theme of "Hindu Rashtra" was borrowed from European fascism along with the now completely discredited theory of eugenics is something we have already mentioned in the previous chapter.

We are claiming that "we" are not Hindus. My claim (as I highlighted in the introduction) is that the Indian fascists are so dumb that they cannot even invent their own terms and borrow from the linguistic baggage of their West Asian neighbours. Of course one should celebrate all possible borrowings, but what we claim is that the Hindu fetish-loving fascist in claiming to be an ultra-nationalist cannot even invent his own terms. We have already mentioned in the second chapter that the original term "Hindu" is of Persian origin. What the Indian fascist does is manipulate this original Persian term and fosters the archaic Brahmanical ritualistic repertoire, especially the caste-stratified system of social control, and place it as a societal whole. By "Hindu" one actually means this archaic ritualism and the imposition of this archaic structure on the Indian masses. That this term was then romanticized by the European Orientalists since William Jones and Max Müller and then taken over by Vivekananda, Aurobindo and Gandhi ought to be emphasized. The Persian geo-political term now becomes a colonial geo-political term. *The term "Hinduism" thus conceals more than it reveals.*

If thus we have two bases of the term "Hinduism": one the archaic and the Brahmanical and the other the Romantic, we also have B.R. Ambedkar's rendering as a social system that is directly in antithesis to democratic principles.

Humanism and Mass Politics

While turning to this theme of identity politics we are arguing for modernity and secular identities where the programme of the annihilation of caste, along with class struggle and the labour question are kept at the base of our argument. We turn to two figures, B.R. Ambedkar and Gandhi to understand this question of forming both archaic and modern identities. In more than one sense we will be arguing against Gandhi and Gandhism. Yet in this arguing against Gandhi it must not be forgotten that

Gandhi as a great democratic figure, is sometimes also equated with Lenin. It is Balibar who has said that "Lenin and Gandhi are the two greatest figures among revolutionary theorist-practitioners of the first half of the 20th century"[2] According to such a reading:

> Both of them, Lenin as well as Gandhi, in different ways undertook the heroic and at the same time adventurous experiment of putting into practice the long cherished dreams of humanity. They were both rooted deeply in their own nations; and their reforms and their methods were entirely the result of the destinies of their countries, of the limitations of Russian and Indian conditions, and that at a moment when both nations had arrived at a turning point in their national development. But the political enterprise of both the Russian and the Hindu goes far beyond the narrow boundaries of the national and the temporary. Russia and India were merely to be the subjects of a great and universally valid experiment whose success was to give an example to the world and to spread the new doctrines of the two reformers over the whole earth. Lenin and Gandhi were upheld by the emotion of an ecstatic faith, the faith that their country, was called to redeem humanity.[3]

We shall argue here that while Gandhi cannot be written off, simply as a sort of an instrument reason in the times of the anti-colonial struggle—our claim is that Gandhi was a Romantic anti-capitalist—I shall argue against Gandhism. While arguing against Gandhism, I shall keep on arguing against the Indian Stalinists and the Established Parliamentary Left that could not understand the deep complexity of the caste-class relations embedded in the Asiatic mode of production, nor could understand Marx's theory of multilinear historicism. However, to those who thought that the philosophy of Ambedkar is not at all applicable to the radical left movement, that he talked of only the Indian caste system without ever talking of modern classes and capitalism, one only needs to recall him: "*Class conflict is the cause of misery*".[4] And to those who think that Gandhi was the apostle of radical change one needs to recall him: *I am working for the cooperation and coordination of capital and labour and of landlords and tenants. Class war is foreign to the essential genius of India. The Ramraja of my dreams ensures the rights equal of prince and pauper.*[5]

Keeping these in mind, we start with a radical reconstruction of left politics. We start with three basic humanist propositions:

(1) Antiquity ushered a revolution initiated by a complex of philosophies—the Babylonians, Egyptians Persians, Indians, Greeks, Chinese—that culminated in the philosophies of Plato and Aristotle followed by Ibn Sina and via the European Enlightenment finally culminating in Hegel. If Aristotle, the "greatest thinker of antiquity", as Marx thought him to be, would bequeath the formal logical system, Hegel, the great student of the French Revolution would have ushered another revolution—that of modern dialectics. We the children of the Age of Reason have these two great logical systems. Marx as we know chooses the latter—dialectics, or dialectical materialism to be precise.

(2) There probably could be no better social scientist and revolutionary than the figure of Ambedkar in India. And like every true and authentic scientist he is essentially political (in the Leninist sense that Althusser outlined in *Lenin and Philosophy*).

(3) The base-superstructure model that Marx talks of is not a reductionist model, not an determinism, where Marx's term *bestimmte* is located as an iron code. Instead, Marx as a historicist and humanist (we know these to be from Antonio Gramsci) locates *bestimmte* or "determination" as the problem of formation. An economic formation thus creates a political and ideological superstructure. And for Marx the humanist, the human being of the here and the now,

> is always central to this historical picture. The problem of ethics is thus always central to Marx.

For him like the rest of the Enlightenment thinkers, a moral regeneration is always the prelude to a real revolution. It is from this space that we argue for searching new spaces whereby the moral bloc (again we know this term is from Gramsci) is created that confronts capitalism. We search for the "we", the "multitude", the people against capitalism and imperialism. So far we see "we-ness" everywhere and yet nowhere. Why is this so?

For that we turn to Laing's idea of the divided self. The divided self has no "I" no "we". Why is this so? To answer this question, we like the rest of the idealist school of transcendental idealism, turn to the most ancient text that locates this ideal-primeval divided self where we note the 10th mandala of the *Rg Veda* which states how society is not only divided into frozen castes-classes, but also emphasizes the ideological monopoly of the upper caste elites. And since the Indian left has not been able to engage the humanist Enlightenment project of the annihilation of caste and capitalism, both caste and capitalist politics haunt every aspect of Indian society. And because the Indian fascists are crying hoarse on the need for the "Hindu nation", we claim that there is both morbidity and necromancy in their very ideological problematic.

Necromancy and Fascism

And it is with this note on necromancy that we once again recall Walter Benjamin's angel of history flying over the ruins of imperialism and the phantasmagoria produced called "Hindu Rashtra".[6] Benjamin's angel sees only ruins below. Let us see what we are able to see. We recall Ambedkar when he talked of the dangers of postponing the moral regeneration that "Hindu society", as he called it, terribly needed. His answer was that only those had gone through a "moral regeneration" and "intellectual regeneration" could go through this process. These same people had to have the convictions "born of intellectual emancipation". His answer was that "Hindu leaders who could are in my opinion quite unfit for this task".[7]

In a very historicist and humanist sense, Ambedkar is talking Marxism, and here I mean Marxism of Marx. And because Gandhi comes into the scene of the discourses of emancipation one is in a certain sense talking of both emancipation and despotism. Both Marx and Ambedkar, one needs to engage, while Gandhi will be put as the theoretical founder of Romantic anti-capitalism, a crypto-Hegelian and Tolstoyean both at the same time, as well as a conservative democrat. Whether he qualifies as what Žižek calls "social fascism" is quite another matter. We place Gandhi as a political democrat, but a social conservative, who for his stubborn refusal to critique the caste system. And it is for this reason, his location as a "social fascist" cannot be dispensed with. After understanding the complexities of Gandhi, one notes what is happening in Indian universities (especially philosophy departments) where the discourse of neo-Hinduism is being actively cultivated. In this sense we agree with what Friedhelm Hardy, in 'A Radical Reassessment of the Vedic Heritage' talked of, namely, the intrinsic connection between Hinduism in the political arena and the Hinduism that Indian academics are trying to produce.

Since Gandhi is probably the guiltiest for rehabilitating both the caste system and Hinduism, we need to turn to this form of what one may call "nativist" discourse. Gandhi is both a native and a nativist, who removes his English suit to become an Asian fakir. He is also the master in learning the art of metamorphosis. Just as Marx's commodity "changes its features, hair and other things, besides", Gandhi's metamorphosis creates what we know today as the "Hindu", the tolerant and suffering Hindu, who sang odes to "Hey Ram". How "Hey Ram" became "Jai Siya Ram" in the discourse of Indian nationalism and how the imagined tolerant and suffering Hindu became a symbolic Hindutvavadi has to be noted. This "Hindu" (both Gandhi's version of the tolerant and suffering Hindu and the extremely intolerant and communal rendering as practised by the Indian fascists) are fictions. If the first storyteller was Gandhi, the new storytellers are the Indian fascists, since both justify the "borders of cruelty" that we earlier mentioned. "Hinduism", one must insist, is an invention. The borders of cruelty, alas, are a brute fact.

Hinduism, one must insist, is inherently woven with caste, and this caste system has to be understood as the alienated "cutting off" of one human from the other governed by the dictatorship of the upper castes.[8] And since Indian democracy did not uproot caste, we call Indian democracy "conservative democracy".[9] We also said that Gandhi has to be seen as the source of Congress conservatism[10] that despite its cosmopolitan appearance remains conservative in actual practice. As Ambedkar said Gandhism is a "call of return to Antiquity" as well as a "reanimation of India's dread, dying past".[11] It is this conservative character that the Indian liberals nurtured, thus disabling the programme of the annihilation of the caste system. What I now say is that the caste system, in the age of late imperialism in permanent crises, structures minorities like the Muslims along with the traditionally oppressed castes to look like the "hellish other" that serves the interests of anti-democratic, anti-secular and pro-imperialist forces. My third point is that caste is to be understood as the Confucian lethargy of Indian civilization which serves the production of the political economy of capitalism-at-the-periphery, as well as the creation of a sluggish de-politicized and fragmented working class that is so internally divided that it cannot play out its role as the insurrectionist proletariat. The conclusion of the above observations is that we need to relate the problem of caste with the divided self and the general regression of thinking.

Since we are contrasting secularism and democracy on the one hand and fascism on the other hand, as well as contrasting science with fiction, let us once again refer to Gandhi. For Gandhi as the whole genre of nativism, India is homogeneous devoid of internal differences and contradictions. For him, India is 'Hindu society', mystical and tolerant. While it is apparent that this form of nativism was born more from the cranium of Orientalism than indigenous Indian thinking, where the discourse of Orientalism—from Anquetil-Duperron, William Jones, Charles Wilkins and Henry Thomas Colebrooke to the German Orientalism of Friedrich Schlegel and Maurice Winternitz—created the early discourse of 'Hinduism', followed faithfully after the defeat of the 1857 revolution against British colonialism by Aurobindo, Vivekananda and Bankim Chandra, one inserts another discourse, the discourse of what I call the "Indian Fanonists" (after Frantz Fanon), the radical democrats, who at least since the 1870s, reinterpreted Indian history from a radically new and different perspective, the radical secularist perspective of humanist history, which means *non-Hindu history,* that called for the transcendence of phantasmagorical mythology. Remember for Ambedkar caste destroys all human feelings. And that is why one needs to tell the Indian fascists who try to create the myth of the "Hindu nation" that "the ideal Hindu must be like a rat living in his own hole refusing to have contact with others. There is an utter lack among the Hindus of what the sociologists call 'consciousness of kind'."[12]

And because we claim to have understood this, we claim a very different account of history. Marx had said somewhere, and we know where, that according to Hegel, history repeats itself as it were twice, "he forgot to add" as Marx says, "the first time as tragedy, the second as farce".[13] Marx, it seems, should have said that history repeats itself thrice, the third time as great joy, since in this third repetition the masses shall be armed with the art of insurrection. In a certain sense we are sitting on the crossroads of history where tragedy, farce and joy appear all at the same time.

Keeping this theme of repeating history, we turn once again to the problem of identifying caste in India, especially in identifying the genealogy of caste. Central to this theme of caste is the question of capitalism and modern classes and whether the new capitalist structures are able to erase the earlier caste-based mode of discrimination. The relation between social hierarchies and graded inequality (the *sine qua non* of the caste system and the philosophy of 'Hinduism') on the one hand, and the very Marxist issue of class struggle, especially the bourgeois/proletariat opposition on the other hand, has to be pointed out once again. Alongside the question of caste and class emerges another issue that of caste and race that we noted in the previous chapter. We thus pose the question: "Is caste and casteism similar to racism, if not a European type of racism, then at least a South Asian type of it?" Finally the problem of caste is also related to the psychoanalytic problem of neurosis and psychosis. It is keeping these three problematic: (1) class, (2) race and racism,[14] and (3) neurosis and psychosis that we shall try to locate the question of how the Indian fascists manipulate caste to produce their ultra-conservative politics. Combined with these three problematic we also deliberate on the question of social and political power in India.

And since the Indian fascists stubbornly want to make hysterical claims of the mythical Hindu nation, one needs to state that there is absolute control over the Ideological and Repressive State Apparatuses where the upper caste elites wield both the Ideological State Apparatus of India and the Repressive State Apparatus (the army, the police and the paramilitary forces). The peasants (the Vaisyas) and the artisans (Shudras) become (to borrow Herbert Marcuse's term from a different context) the proletarianized "Great Refusal".

A slight historical reflection flows from the sighting of this basic structure of social stratification and why what we now know as "Hinduism" has a fetish for hierarchy based on the law of purity and pollution. A small note is necessary. Though radical subalterns have continuously challenged caste, even modified it in many ways, it has not been overthrown, or as Ambedkar said "annihilated". Like the neurotic who negates the trauma, only to posit it once again, caste refuses to leave the scene of India. This is because those who control the neurotic Ideological State Apparatus of India are the uncanny elites who somehow make us recall Shakespeare's Cassius who was noted by Caesar with a lean and hungry look, who thinks too much. And as Caesar once noted: "Such men are dangerous".[15] We live not only with dangerous people. We live in the era of danger. This era of danger encompasses tragedy, farce and joy. The first two acts: tragedy and farce are of the silent counterrevolution, of the neurotic returning again and again. Let us have a look at this neurotic and the struggle against this neurosis.

The Return of the Emancipated

In more than one way we recall Žižek, especially with his remembering, if not rehabilitation of Lenin. We begin with the outburst of sarcastic laughter that he talks of in his essay, 'A Plea for Leninist Intolerance', where he says that the bourgeoisie which declared Marx to be dead, now talk of Marx, the so-called pioneer of culture studies, but never Lenin. We then go to a quote from Saint-Just that Žižek notes: "That which produces the general good is always terrible". With this theme in mind we go to the articulation on the discourse of emancipation, especially on Marxism and the question of communism. And because Gandhi does somehow almost surreptitiously enters in the rather strange discourse of emancipation, and because Ambedkar is always, and rightly so, tauntingly haunting the ghost of Gandhi and his followers, we in a very provocative and realist way say: we are not Hindus. But why, so one may ask, has this being Hindu and not being Hindu, have to do anything with emancipation?

Now this non-Hindu account of politics has to be related to

historicism and humanism, the narratives of modes of production and class struggle constituted within the concrete issues of caste and the Asiatic mode of production, not to forget the most celebrated Leninist theme of understanding insurrection as art. We talk thus of philosophy, to be precise Marxist philosophy, a philosophy that is essential political. We thus raise the question: how is free humanity possible?, a freedom that is learnt in the practice of insurrection as art.

It must be noted that the critique of Indian fascism has to be based on Marx's *Economic and Philosophic Manuscript of 1844* (which brings in the questions of capitalist alienation) along with *Capital* and the rather ignored *Ethnological Notebooks*. Unlike the Established Left in India, we argue for a multilinear historicism and a politics of permanent revolution through the art of insurrection where we learn to skip the bourgeois stage altogether. Unlike the Established Left that ignores caste, and if they think of it, then it was sort of post-Marxist, post-modernist borrowing, we concretely relate caste with modern classes and political power.

So how does Marxism-Leninism differ from the Established Left, especially the Parliamentary Left? It differs completely in the approach to Indian history because it totally disregards their theory of "Indian feudalism", their theory of transition from so-called feudalism to capitalism, their understanding of caste as a mere 'feudal' remnant along with the dialectics of caste-class. In antithesis to this petty bourgeois Established Left we state the following:

1. To construct a foundation for radical people's movement that we call the "Asian Soviets". These Asian Soviets confront not only imperialism, capitalism and its essential pre-capitalist structures (we will not call these mere remnants, but essential structures for contemporary global accumulation of capital), but also confront the nation state and its

ruling ideology of neo-liberalism.

2. One then goes beyond the discourses of "iron laws" of history as well as go beyond the discipline of ideology for the politics of radical praxis and the New Discipline of desireology.
3. From this New Terrain discovered we also move away from the spaces of civil society and the state into the New Terrain of the "commons".

The "commons", as one can decipher from the word itself, is in contrast to class fragmentation. But more than the modern class system it gets in contradiction with the caste system whose very essence is inequality and slavery. And it is in this site of the commons that Revolutionary Marxism initiates the Cultural Revolution, the revolution that would serve as the actuality of the revolution. We claim that this Cultural Revolution needs a dramaturgy inspired by Ambedkar's critique of Hinduism. Marxist science now becomes a dramaturgy. For understanding how science becomes a dramaturgy, how science, politics and aesthetics meet, one will have to talk of Marx's idea of science as *human natural science*, where Marx discovers not only the new continent of history, but also discovers the science of understanding human alienation and the fetishes produced thereof.[16] Marx here discovers a New Physics, and thus discovers a New Space that has transcended class societies. There are three terms which hint to this New Space discovered which critiques all class and caste stratified societies:

(1) the human essence (*das menschliche Wesen*),

(2) *Gattungswesen* (species being) where humanity is understood as a species that seeks equality, liberty and fraternity, and

(3) the celebrated "commons" or what Engels called *Gemeinwesen* (literally translated as "the common essence", known to the world as the Paris Commune).

It is this New Space—that of the commons—that one needs to

recognize and understand. The commons is the future of India, a future that is inexorably tied to the future of the world. The struggle against fascism shall have to be fought in this space of the commons.

REFERENCES

1. Karl Marx, 'A Contribution to the Critique of Hegel's Philosophy of Right. Introduction', in *Karl Marx. Early Writings*, trans. Rodney Livingstone and Gregor Benton (London: Penguin Books, 1992), p. 243.
2. Etienne Balibar, 'Lenin and Gandhi: A Missed Encounter', in *Radical Philosophy*, 172, March/April, 2012. Also see René Fülöp-Miller's *Lenin and Gandhi*, trans. F.S. Flint and D.F. Tait (London & New York: G.P. Putnam's Sons, 1927).
3. René Fülöp-Miller, *Lenin and Gandhi*, trans. F.S. Flint and D.F. Tait (London & New York: G.P. Putnam's Sons, 1927), p. VII.
4. B.R. Ambedkar, 'Buddha or Karl Marx', in *Dr. Babasaheb Ambedkar. Writings and Speeches*, Vol. 3 (Pune: Education Department, Government of Maharashtra, 1987).
5. M.K. Gandhi, 'Answers to Zamindars, July 25, 1934', in *The Penguin Gandhi Reader*, ed. Rudrangshu Mukherjee (New Delhi: Penguin Books, 1993), p. 238.
6. Walter Benjamin, 'Theses on the Philosophy of History', in *Illuminations*, trans. Harry Zohn (Glasgow: Fontana/Collins, 1979), pp. 259-60.
7. B.R. Ambedkar, 'Reply to the Mahatma', in *The Essential Writings of B.R. Ambedkar*, ed. Valerian Rodrigues (New Delhi: Oxford University Press, 2008), p. 217.
8. See my 'Asking Questions of Caste, Class and History to the Indian Left', in *Radical Socialist*, May 18, 2012.
9. Christophe Jaffrelot, *India's Silent Revolution. The Rise of the Low Castes in North Indian Politics* (Delhi: Permanent Black, 2003), pp. 11-2.
10. Ibid., pp. 13-47.
11. B.R. Ambedkar, 'Gandhism', in *The Essential Writings of B.R. Ambedkar*, ed. Valerian Rodrigues (New Delhi: Oxford University Press, 2008), p. 165.
12. B.R. Ambedkar, 'Annihilation of Caste', in *The Essential Writings*

of B.R. Ambedkar, ed. Valerian Rodrigues (New Delhi: Oxford University Press, 2008), p. 267.

13. Karl Marx, 'The Eighteenth Brumaire of Louis Bonaparte', in *Marx Engels. Selected Works* (Moscow: Progress Publishers, 1975), p. 96.
14. The cultural and economical subordination of the Dalits emerges from this Indian form of racism.
15. William Shakespeare, 'Julius Caesar', in *The Complete Works of William Shakespeare* (London: Henry Pordes, 1983), Act I, Sc II, p. 890.
16. Karl Marx, *Economic and Philosophic Manuscripts of 1844* (Moscow: Progress Publishers, 1982), pp. 98-9.

5

Why We Can Never Be Hindus: The Struggle Against Fascism in India

Every rise of fascism bears witness to a failed revolution.

Walter Benjamin

Now in your own interest and in the interest of this great country you must learn to listen and to read what we say. A people who refuse to listen to new questions and learn new answers will perish and not prosper.

Kancha Ilaiah

Whose sentiments are really being hurt? Are we going to stagnate as a culture that continuously touches the feet of intolerance?

Stephen Alter

Fascism the Death of the "Commons"

Since the late 1980s the "commons" and the culture of the popular classes ceased to be mobilized by democratic forces. The Established Left obsessed with mere trade unionism regressed into a form of notorious economism, leaving the arena of popular culture for bourgeois forces to be mobilized. It was the Hindu right in the era of triumphant Thatcherism and the rise of the global neo-cons, who were able to take a lead in the capture of the "commons". Both the Congress with its policies of pragmatic and competitive communalism and the RSS with its programmatic and pogromatic communalism were competing for the space for capturing the space for the emergence of the Hindu right. The "commons" ceased to be the "commons". Instead it became the site of the rise of the anti-Muslim movement in Ayodhya. The Hindutva fascist horde would emerge as the "inverted commons".

The rise of the BJP as a hegemonic political force was however built not only on the communal-fascist work of the RSS, but aided by the opportunist policies of the Congress. The role of the formation of the Shiv Sena in the 1960s to fight the communists in the city of Bombay (now Mumbai) and later in propelling an unknown priest Jarnail Singh Bhindranwale in Punjab to counter the Akalis are two examples that for the Congress, one was a secularist only in words and totally chauvinist in deeds. The Hindutvavadi warriors would not merely be riding the horse of neo-liberal capitalism, but also riding the horses trained by the liberal democratic Congress. What General Zia-ul-Haq would do to Pakistan and Ayatollah Khomeini would do to Iran; the RSS would do to India. The "commons" would not be the site of Dalit and workers' struggles. Instead as the "inverted commons", it would turn out to be the death knell for people's struggles.

Fascism and the Phule-Ambedkarite Cultural Revolution

Religious fascism, whether Pakistani, Iranian or Indian, is built on areas of culture where manipulability of popular symbols leads to their conversion into ritual functions which leads, on the one hand, to the formation of a totalitarian state, the personality cult, the hatred of religious minorities and the cult of riots and wars; and on the other hand leads to the sanctioning of these into the form of what Walter Benjamin calls the "aura".[1] And with religious fascism surrounded by this aura, a rational understanding is largely forgotten for a collective form of hysteria. What happens with this form of religious fascism is not so much the rendering of politics as some form of aesthetics,[2] but what happens is the de-politicization of politics and then its reification into a hysterical symbol. Fascism then does not aestheticize politics (this was Benjamin's stand), it makes politics hysterical. *Communism responds by politicizing hysteria.*[3]

It is from this epistemic space where one claims that one needs a much larger nodal point to enter the space of popular democratic politics in India (especially a nodal point when democracy is continuously being discredited by the RSS Parvivar, and fascism and the ideology of a totalitarian managerial state are celebrated) than the mere nodal spaces of economism and parliamentarism. And since this managerial totalitarian state claims the status of an anti-secular Hindu state, modelled after the classical European fascist state, the demand for a popular democratic politics of the popular classes becomes more urgent. And if this emergence of a fascist state is becoming obvious with the construction of the image of a totalitarian messianic leader, the question remains as to what is to be the nature of this politics of the popular classes that come into the scene of action that is able to disrupt the hegemony of the fascist elite.

We begin with where we left off in the previous chapter: 'Why We Are Not Hindus: A Reply to the Indian Fascists'. We start with the proposition of classical Marxism that while fascist politics is driven by the logic of late imperialism in permanent crisis, we take up Arthur Rosenberg and Jairus Banaji's propositions that fascism is a mass movement having popular support.[4] And since we hear once again of the alleged splendour of Hinduism from the cacophonous media industry set up by the RSS, and also since we hear that the Indian fascists are going to restore the illusory pride of the once-upon-a-time "India living in the Golden Age" after the crown of parliamentary democracy is placed on the head of the Minister of Genocide, we need not only critique the fascist politics of "Hindutva", but we also need to recall Jyotiba Phule and B.R. Ambedkar on the phantasmagorical character of Hinduism. Thus we need not merely say to the fascists that their idea of *political Hinduism* is total nonsense, but we also need to say the same about *Hinduism proper*.

This chapter is both on the critique of *political Hinduism* and *Hinduism proper*. Our argument claims that Hinduism (in whatever form) is not an exotic religion of the "splendour of the marvellous east" (as the Orientalists thought it to be), but the ideology of petty commodity production and that genuine democracy is impossible when caste and its religious weapon called "Hinduism" exist. That Hinduism has lived on even in the era of modernity is the tragedy of Indian history. Our argument is also based on the line of reasoning that the Communist Revolution has to understand the Phule-Ambedkarite Revolution.

It is thus that one can say that the Phule-Ambedkarite Cultural Revolution has to be a necessary part of the Communist Revolution. What the European Enlightenment was to the European revolutions, the Phule-Ambedkarite Cultural Revolution is to India. Here we are replacing the traditional term used by the Established Left, namely "bourgeois democratic revolution" with the idea of the Phule-Ambedkarite Cultural Revolution. What we are implying here is that early capitalism in India coming in the form of colonial capitalism abandoned the revolutionary legacy that was embedded in the European revolutions especially of the 1789 French Revolution. This makes us rethink the idea of the bourgeois democratic revolution and its role in India. This also leads us to re-think the project of parliamentary democracy which itself leads us to re-think the questioning of Indian liberalism, their almost stubborn refusal to annihilate caste and their refusal to directly fight the fascist RSS. What is meant by the Phule-Ambedkarite Cultural Revolution is the reminder to the radical left that the Indian bourgeoisie could not continue and complete the anti-feudal revolution that it was supposed to do, since it was embedded deeply within India's pre-capitalist formations.

There has to be a word of caution: this Phule-Ambedkarite

Cultural Revolution is not a form of the Indian bourgeois democratic revolution. Yes it is an anti-feudal Cultural Revolution, but a revolution that is not bourgeois in nature. It has to be socialist through and through. In fact one will have to state that not only India, but all of South Asia will have to go through an anti-feudal, anti-capitalist and anti-imperialist Cultural Revolution, a revolution that synchronizes *immediately* with the Communist Revolution. There are not going to be stages as has been imagined by forms of left politics: the bourgeois democratic revolution followed by the socialist revolution. In fact the latter will operate in terms of a form of simultaneity, a form of a revolution in permanence. Thus, what one also needs to say is that, there can be no bourgeois democratic revolution for India. And this is because capitalism in India has failed, and will continue to fail to universalize, fail to perform the historical (anti-feudal) task that it executed in Western Europe. Capitalism in India is not the capitalism that emerged in Western Europe. It does not have within its cranium a form of Protestant ethic and the spirit of rational inquiry. What happens in India (as in South Asia) is that the Protestant ethic and the spirit of rational inquiry would live side by side with caste-based ethics and the spirit of total irrationality. Indian modernity would be a kitsch between these two: the rational and the irrational. What we have in India is neither pure capitalism, nor pure feudalism, but what we may call *"feudo-capitalism"*, a particular mode of production that developed with the coming of colonial capital. The mode of production prior to the coming of colonialism was the Asiatic mode of production with the caste mode being the main vehicle of extraction of surplus. *In this sense, one has to note that there is nothing called "Indian feudalism". There is however something called "cultural and political feudalism in India" based on caste-apartheid and the system of cultural dependency.*

Therefore we must insist that when we are using the term "feudalism", we are implying something very different from what thinkers from D.D. Kosambi to R.S. Sharma and Irfan Habib meant. "Feudalism" in our sense is a subset of the larger Asiatic mode of production that Marx talked of. What we call "feudal" (in relation to Hinduism and the emergence of fascist forces) is a cultural concept, not an economic one. The concept of "feudo-capitalism", on the other hand, is constituted within the Marxist critique of political economy and thus applies to both the economic base as well as to the political and ideological superstructure.

And this is where the narrative of Hinduism comes in. The main line of argument goes thus: Hinduism that was part of the ideology of the dominant castes in pre-capitalist India is now being nurtured by the Indian bourgeoisie and its culture industry. This culture industry of manufacturing Hinduism has now led to the construction of political Hinduism. And since the anti-caste and anti-feudal revolution was not completed in India (as in South Asia in general), the phantasmagoria of Hinduism keeps rising again and again. The Phule-Ambedkarite Cultural Revolution has to deal with the anti-feudal revolution as also with the construction of Revolutionary Marxism in India. The production of revolutionary agency—the subject of the Indian revolution—shall be its main focus. *Strictly then we must talk of the Marxist-Phule-Ambedkarite Cultural Revolution.*

It is in this perspective that first, we claim (in classical Marxist style) that the community of free human beings precedes everything else. Thus it also claims that the triad of liberty-equality-fraternity is central to this politics of human emancipation, a triad that is lacking in both the Asiatic-feudal societies and in what one may call "Hinduism as such". Second, we claim that the very idea of a "Hindu society" is a total myth. (There can be "Indian society" but not "Hindu society"). The second point that locates the mythical status of Hindu society is constituted in the great contribution of both Phule and Ambedkar. Understanding the contours of this logic of de-ritualization (a logic borrowed from Benjamin), one understands that Hinduism is most certainly not the religion of tolerance and peace that we are made to believe.[5] It is what has recently been pointed out as "the toleration of intolerance,"[6] where humans are considered "more bestial than beasts".[7] It is devoid of the public spirit and shorn of all ethics.[8] It is what Jyotiba Phule called a "greedy religion" of the "unscrupulous beggars": the cunning Brahmans and Bhats—the ritualistic priests of totalitarian dominance.[9] This contextualizing of the cultural politics of Hinduism in the radical politics of Phule and Ambedkar is of great importance for democratic politics in India. It is this duo who will serve as the main politico-cultural battle with the Indian fascists.

Let us begin with the myth of tolerance in Hinduism, a myth that runs from Gandhi to Amartya Sen, a myth that has been exploited both by the Indian liberals and fascists:

> Tolerance, of course, is an English word, expressing the outsiders' view of what they think happens in India. There is no word in any of the Indian languages that corresponds to the English term 'religious tolerance', which covers everything from mere 'endurance of' or 'putting up with' religious difference (as one 'tolerates' pain) to a more active endorsement, even celebration of religious difference....There is no Sanskrit or Hindi word for 'tolerance' in that sense, as a good to be sought in the world; there are words only for passive and negative words for endurance.[10]

This chapter is thus, at the same time, a political attack on not only the proponents of Hindutva, but also an attack on the Indian liberal democrats. The question of not being Hindus is then transformed into the ethical question of never wanting to be Hindus. We thus begin with the question of religion, namely the question of Hinduism that Ambedkar had critiqued as the worst form of anti-humanism that could ever be found. We begin however with the questions: "Why does one say that the critique of religion is the prerequisite of all critiques"[11], and how does one concretize this critique in radical politics?" And since we have been told by the political right in India that the Indian state ought to be a "Hindu state", we are concretely setting the agenda of revolutionary politics to understand the possible alternatives to not only the fascism of the Hindutva Parivar, but also the politics of liberal democracy that is itself nurturing this form of fascism. Our concern is democracy, and by democracy we mean *real democracy*, not formal democracy that parliamentary democracy advocates.

Let us continue with our proposition that if "Hinduism proper" or "Hinduism as such" (as a homologous and monological school of thought) is a myth, then the politics of Hinduism and Hindutvavadi are greater myths as they are both based on false and illusory premises. Consider Ambedkar on the mythical character of Hinduism:

> The first and foremost thing that must be recognized is that Hindu society is a myth. The name Hindu is itself a foreign name....Hindu society as such does not exist. It is only a collection of castes.....A caste has no feeling that it is affiliated to other castes except when there is a Hindu-Muslim riot.[12]

This is the first thing that one needs to tell the masses. Hinduism as such, i.e. as a rational societal order or a rational doctrine of the Indian masses does not exist. And yet Hinduism exists—exists as an irrational cluster of castes and even as an irrational doctrine. The summary is that what we may call "Hinduism as we know it" is nothing but the rule by totalitarian force of the upper castes. There is another issue that Ambedkar raises: the almost psychotic character of Hinduism, where people trapped in the iron cage of this political and culture industry get to be totally oblivious to the objective world, especially totally oblivious to the sufferings of humanity. According to this logic, people have no qualms about a Minister of Genocide becoming the Prime Minister. Consider Ambedkar once again:

> Why is the Hindu so indifferent? In my opinion this indifferentism is the result of the caste system which has made *Sanghatan* and cooperation even for a good cause impossible.[13]

That this passage corresponds to the one made by Marx in his celebrated 'The British Rule in India' where he talks of the alienated or what he calls "idyllic village communities" that are not only the solid foundation of "Oriental despotism", but where these stratified communities restrain the human mind, enslaving people "beneath traditional rules" devoid of "all grandeur and historical energies" worshipping animals and hating humanity;[14] with those of Ambedkar should be highlighted. Also the fact that Ambedkar's definition of caste as "enclosed class" corresponds to Marx's view of caste as "petrified and ossified guilds"[15] should also be highlighted.

The central issue is how these estranged communities governed by the logic of lordship and bondage have made cooperation for a good cause impossible, but have made the corporate fascist state possible. This is the tragedy of Indian history.

Modern Hinduism as the Imagined Signifier

It must be noted that by "Hinduism"' we imply the very concrete context that Ambedkar worked in, a context that is determined by caste-hegemony. While our understanding is built on rigorous forms of Revolutionary Marxism, we will also be involving what we call a "Marxist-Ambedkarite" understanding of social formations in India and the role of the Indian liberal state. In this sense we are revisiting the sites of radical praxis—of a re-invention of a radical left in the age of neo-liberalism. Again in more than one sense we are re-visiting the sites of extremely serious social sciences, a seriousness where the voice of radical subalternism of what I call "Marxist-Ambedkarism" is heard.

This brings us to the first of our propositions: there can be no real revolution without a Cultural Revolution where the old anti-humanist morality determined by the class-caste system is transcended. In a very Ambedkarite sense it also means that this Cultural Revolution needs a transcendence of not only the caste system with its absolutely outdated sense of morals, but needs a transcendence of what one calls "Hinduism" itself.

This is what the Phule-Ambedkarite Revolution with a Revolution says: "Hinduism, as we know", since the last century, has to deal not merely with the Romantic idealism of the European Orientalists, not only with indigenous Indian traditions, but now primarily has to deal with the warrior-priest imagination (heralded by Savarkar and Golwalkar and now practised by the RSS). To those who think that Hinduism is an innocent doctrine as found in the works from Schelling and Winternitz to Vivekananda and Gandhi, it must be noted that the Nazis took Vedic Hinduism very seriously and Heinrich Himmler (the notorious Nazi Reichsführer) was a devout follower of esoteric and occultist Hinduism where aided by Houston Stewart Chamberlain he stressed the warrior interpretation of Indian history. One must note that Himmler imagined himself to be Arjuna and Hitler as Krishna. It must also be noted that the Brahman-Kshatriya (priest-warrior) base will remain as the core of both these versions—the Romantic and the fascist.

One needs to highlight two things. First, that the Indo-Iranian genealogy of "Hinduism" is forgotten by the Indian fascists and a bizarre form of cultic-territorial nationalism is constructed. This point was repeatedly stressed by Phule who condemned all types of Hindu nationalism as forms of pretentious nationalism, while stressing that the Brahmans were descendants of the Indo-Iranian warring tribesmen who attacked and colonized India with their bizarre type of caste hierarchy, ideology of ritualism, patriarchy and anti-humanism. Second, the origins of the caste marker in Hinduism lie in the 10th mandala of the *Rg Veda* where a certain form of not only class and race-based stratification, but also a form of schizophrenia was written on its banners. And since we have been told, more than once by the established order of things, that "we", the "we" that comprises the Indian nation state is basically the "we-ness" of Hinduism, the "we-ness" that is said to lie as the metaphysical basis of so-called "Indian civilization", we turn once more to the seriousness of the site of radical praxis that seeks to overthrow this "we-ness" of classes-castes along with its inherent racism and schizophrenia. If the Indian collective is said to be a "Hindu collective", then it is truly a false collective, a collective that refuses to think. Consider the foundational myth of both caste stratification as well as Hinduism where the Brahmans are said to be the mouth while the other social groups are said to be the arms, thighs, feet and other unmentioned parts. The foundational myth does not talk of the brain or the heart. It thus does not (and cannot) talk of thinking and feeling. Take this case and relate it with Ambedkar's radical thesis of a Cultural Revolution not only against the social structures of caste stratification, but also against the system called "Hinduism" that protects and nurtures not only this form of stratification, but all forms of stratification in India and all forms of Indian regressive thinking.

The point therefore is to study the false sense of the "Hindu collective" that makes impossible the construction of an "Indian collective", a true collective where the unity of the popular classes is possible. It is also a critique of this false sense of Indian liberalism, especially on the parliamentary system that protects and nurtures this false collective. In this sense we agree with another observation of Žižek that "fidelity to the democratic consensus means the acceptance of the present liberal-parliamentary consensus, which precludes any serious questioning of how this liberal-democratic order is complicit in the phenomena it officially condemns and, of course, any serious attempt to imagine a society whose socio-political order would be different.[16] In this revolutionary space one also needs to locate the revolutionary spirit of Ambedkar who had said that:

> There is great need of someone with sufficient courage to tell Indians: 'Beware of parliamentary democracy; it is not the best product as it appears to be.'[17]

What one needs to do is develop a new revolutionary science where critique of Hinduism as a false collective is simultaneous with the critique of both liberal democracy and caste.[18]

What one needs to do is to put caste as the central category in Marxist historiography, caste located in the problematic of the Asiatic mode of production, caste that has yet not left us even in the age of late capitalism. And that is why we also insist that the philosophies of Marx and Ambedkar are central in this analysis. But since we talk of caste as not yet leaving us in the age of late capitalism, we also recall Freud's theory of neurosis as the eternal recurrence of the self-same trauma. As we shall see in the course of this chapter, since critics of Marx (especially those following Edward Said) found that Marx's critique of pre-capitalist India as stagnant was some sort of hidden Orientalism based on the Eurocentric narrative; we shall be relating the Freudian critique of neurosis to critique the Indian caste system. Thus when Marx had talked of the Indian "self-sufficient communities that constantly reproduce themselves in the same form, and when accidentally destroyed, spring up again on the spot and with the same name",[19] we were referring to the *neurotic caste system.*

Here we would like to note that Marx did not think of the so-called "Eastern world" as "timeless" and "devoid of history". Marx not only considers the dynamics of non-European societies, but also emphasizes it. Remember that in the letter to Vera Zasulich he talks of the dynamism of the Russian communes, how they are revolutionary and can directly skip the capitalist mode of production, and thus how one literally has to celebrate the archaic world.[20] Likewise Kosambi too did not view the Indian village in the Orientalist phantasmagoric space of living "outside history". Instead he says how historical materialism links the formation of caste with agricultural economy, and thus in his view was a "tremendous advance in the mode of production".[21] But with this "tremendous revolution" is tied "grimmest poverty and helplessness".[22] What

Kosambi misses out is linking of caste with the Indian variant of the Asiatic mode of production. There is also a lacuna in articulating the superstructural aspect of caste, not to forget his almost forgetfulness of psychoanalysis and his consequent amnesia on the relation between neurosis and caste. We, on the contrary, place this neurosis central to India.

And this neurosis I have scripted in the following tragedy: that caste survived Buddhism, survived Islam and would soon collide with not only colonialism, but also with industrial civilization and modernity, and survive these too. Our repertoire is thus based on the trio—Marx, Freud and Ambedkar. Not only do we relate the Marxist-Freudian-Ambedkarite critique of caste with domination and neurosis, but we also talk of caste as a form of *estranged clannishness* and thus relate it with Marx's theory of alienation. Consequently we talk of caste consciousness with what Hegel and Marx called (in different contexts) as the "unhappy consciousness" and the "estranged mind". Hindutva fascism is an outcome of this unhappy estranged mind.

In a certain sense it is almost necessary to talk of the necessary Dalitization of Marxism and consequently the necessary humanization of the communist movement. It is also necessary to talk of a philosophical rendering of historical materialism where Marx's idea of communism as humanism and naturalism combined with Lenin's praxis of insurrection as art is used to deconstruct caste consciousness.

We once again stress Ambedkar's analysis of both caste as well as its fuzzy and phantasmagorical-ideological superstructure called "Hinduism", where we not only present the inherent psychotic and mythical character of the ideology of pre-capitalist India (innocently called "Hinduism").[23] The psychotic character was mentioned by both Marx in his 1850 articles on India, as well as by Ambedkar.

Now it seems to be tragic that though Ambedkar speaks with the head and the heart of a radical Marxist, the left could simply not understand him. And despite thinkers like

Debiprasad Chattopadhyaya, the Established Left could not unleash a radical historicist and humanist critique of the Indian ruling classes and its ideology called "Hinduism". And since India (alongside a large part of South Asia) did not go through the process of a successful Enlightenment where humanism and science could displace superstition, rituals and anti-humanism inherent in pre-capitalist societies, one has the ghosts of inherited evils still oppressing us, where we are yet seized by the dead! The ghosts are divided into two schools—the liberal and the fascist.

We know of course that the ideology of Hindutva is a concoction and a political fairy tale borrowed more from European fascism than was 'indigenous' to India. Here one needs to point out that not only is this fascist theme incorrect, that not only is the liberal theme of Gandhi and Nehru of an imagined liberal "Hinduism" incorrect, not only the high idealism of Vivekananda and Aurobindo completely wrong in trying to articulate what "India" and "Indianness" means, but also contemporary thinkers like Ashis Nandy alongside the now proliferating departments in American universities, who following the New Orientalists like David Lorenzen hypostasize India as some sort of phantasmagorical "Hindu nation" that has existed from time immemorial with its idealist systems of philosophy that are resistant to secular ideals. That Andres Brevik, the Butcher of Norway also follows this line of thinking and also the fact that the Nazis were readers of the Vedas and the Upanishads should not go unnoticed. Thinkers like David Frawley, a born-again Yankee neo-Hindu who in his *Universal Hinduism: Towards a New Vision* creates a fiction of a great and tolerant Hinduism, completely forgets that "Hinduism" as a discipline is basically a colonial construct that is completely oblivious to caste stratification. One must point out that the now fashionable idea of Hinduism as an eternal religion (*sanatana dharma*) was born only with the 19th century theosophists. And that is why one insists that "the notion of

"Hinduism" is itself a Western-inspired abstraction",[24] an abstraction that completely forgets caste only to hypostasize a so-called tolerant Hinduism. A brief history of the genealogy of the word "Hinduism" is necessary.

For we have not only thinkers from Gandhi to Nandy who reconstruct this hysterical melancholia called "Hinduism" in the repertoire of liberalism, or Lorenzen who constructs this imaginary discourse called "Hinduism" to be taught in American and European universities.[25] We are now not only accompanied by these so-called innocent inventors of imagined discourses. We have now Western academia who accompanies the Indian fascists. Consider Koenard Elst who not only wrote ideological treatises as in his infamous *Decolonizing the Hindu Mind*, but also hate literature like *Rama Janmabhoomi vs. Babri Masjid*, a book that was released by the Indian fascist leader L.K. Advani. And that is why we insist that "Hinduism" is no longer an innocent discourse that can claim to be the most original Gnostic philosophy and neo-Platonism where Ananda Coomaraswamy and Rene Guenon occupy this space of Oriental innocence. It now becomes outrightly fascist, where its inheritors can only be Advani and Narendra Modi, not to forget Andres Brevik, the infamous butcher of Norway. So one may ask: what is so specific to the discourse of "Hinduism" that caste which remains at the essence of its repertoire is almost always perpetually veiled?

And since the Indian fascists want to build their phantasy on the myth of "Hindu Rashtra", we once again chide them for their very unoriginal stupidity. And that is why we have said throughout this book that the term "Hinduism" as is being used today is basically a vacuous and fuzzy term manipulated firstly by the colonial state and then by the upper caste elites in independent India. We have earlier noted earlier that the contemporary usage cannot be confused with the original Persian term that was essentially a geo-cultural term. The present term is completely fetishized and has now become a geo-political term in service to the imperialists.

This fetishized reading not only encompassed the Indian Orientalists who indigenized Max Müller's theory: from Dayananda Saraswati, Bankim Chattopadhyaya, Aurobindo and Vivekananda to Tilak, Lajpat Rai, Savarkar and Gandhi. This fetishized manufacturing of traditions was used by the Indian National Congress since the beginning of the 20th century, which via Nehru got transformed into the Indian variant of political liberalism. What we inherit today is less of the original geo-cultural understanding and more of the geo-political inheritance of colonialism. The tragedy of India is that the radical left (despite Phule, Ambedkar and Annabhau Sathe and the grassroot fighters of liberty, equality and fraternity) has not been able to shake off this phantasmagoria of "Hinduism".

Hindu Rashtra as the Psychotic Symptom of Late Capitalism

The point now is to understand how the RSS has been able to mould this phantasmagoria in order to create the phantom of the imagined "Hindu Rashtra". Thus how the ideology of the Hindu Rashtra becomes a symptom and fetish of an underlying anti-democratic social system is the point that one now needs to analyze. We saw how modern Hinduism appears as the strange creature, part hedgehog, part tortoise. The point now is to see how it then transforms itself into the even stranger creature: the fascist leader in the form of the Hindu superman (Narendra Modi). This symptom/fetish called the "Hindu Rashtra" is similar to Kafka's *Metamorphosis* where the hero, the travelling salesman, Gregor Samsa, is transformed into a terrible insect. The difference between the Kafkaesque narrative and Indian fascism is that the Indian fascist is happy in becoming a strange creature.

That this transformation into a terrible insect called "Hindutva" took place in the late 1980s has to be noted, especially with the role of television in viewing the serial Ramayana. This form of pop Ramayana was instrumental in erasing the local indigenous traditions of what Doniger calls "many Ramayanas"[26] for a singular monistic ideal constructed on the model of the modern capitalist nation state. The fact that since May 2014 Gandhi as the icon of the Indian nation is being replaced by Godse is an example of the metamorphosis into the terrible insect, where this terrible insect as the "Hindu superman" would now have (to recall Sumit Sarkar) total "control over the writing of history"[27].

Philosophically this form of conversion of humanity into some strange creature is decoded in the text of the value form that Marx outlines in *Capital* where the process of metamorphosis of commodities determined by the trio: (1) alienation (implying the loss of humanity), (2) reification (meaning a form of "thingfication" or the de-humanization of humanity), (3) fetishism (or the succumbing of humanity to this monstrous thing) rules the roost not only in market economies, but also in the ideological practices of post-colonial nation states. We say that in capitalism and the production of commodities, there is a loss of human and material form and the production of a *dubious double* where a type of a monstrous machine is produced that itself creates another double that Marx calls the "ghost".[28] What neo-liberal capitalism did since the last two decades in India is that it unleashed both the monstrous ghost of monetarist economics as well as the ghost of communal-fascism.

Now we have just said that this entire discourse called "Hinduism" is a both very political (in the very right-wing sense) as well as very fuzzy. Taking Ambedkar, we say that it is not merely a right-wing fuzzy myth, but also a form of psychosis since it involves an almost withdrawal from reality. Consider this case of what psychoanalysis may call "Hindu psychosis":

> The ideal Hindu must be like a rat living in his own hole refusing to have contact with others. There is an utter lack among the Hindus of what the sociologists call 'consciousness of kind'. There is no Hindu consciousness of kind. In every Hindu the

> consciousness that exists is the consciousness of his caste. That is the reason why the Hindus cannot be considered to form a society or nation.[29]

One then needs to ask: "If Hinduism is a fuzzy right-wing myth with it deeply embedded psychotic character, then why would one not want to be identified with this fuzzy mythical character, a la Narendra Modi as some sort of crazed messiah who has just emerged from the rat hole that Ambedkar pointed out?" There are two basic explanations: one that takes us back to the 10th mandala of the *Rg Veda* that serves as the foundational myth of the caste system where caste implies estranged clannishness + class + race + neurosis-psychosis-schizophrenia.[30] From this psychoanalytic observation of caste and from Ambedkar's observation that Hindus can in no way form a nation, we move to the late 19th and early 20th century observations on political Hinduism. Note three observations: the first by Aurobindo, the second by Keshab Chunder Sen and the third by Vivekananda:

> Nationalism is not a mere political programme. Nationalism is a religion that has come from God. If you are going to be a nationalist, if you are going to assent to this religion of nationalism, you must do it in the religious spirit. When it is said that India shall expand and extend itself, it is the *Sanatan Dharma* that shall expand and extend itself over the world.[31]

> In the advent of the English nation in India we see a reunion of parted cousins, the descent of different families of the ancient Aryan race.[32]

And:

> This is the great ideal before us and everyone must be ready for it—the conquest of the whole world by India. We must go out, we must conquer the world through our spirituality and philosophy.[33]

Consider the classical psychoanalytic understanding of psychosis as the complete withdrawal from reality. Consider how the psychotic now completely deranged, completely oblivious to both the political economy and culture of poverty fantasizes on the fascist conquest of the world. Consider also how this fantasy of the Hindu superman embodied in the mythical figure of Narendra Modi creates and recreates the borders of cruelty. The point now is to understand how these borders of cruelty create new untouchables, new forms of exclusions and new forms of alienation. The new forms of exclusion are based on the fascist's hatred for progressive thought, based on the complete manipulability of the mind and the falsification of history.

But this fascist form of exclusion, while emerging from caste-stratified society, is re-vitalized by a basic liberal understanding of history—namely that history (rather bourgeois history) will progress—leading to the bizarre type of "end of history" that Francis Fukuyama talked of, where neo-liberal capitalism will bring in peace and prosperity. But this form of fantasized myth of development where an equal fantasy of inclusion is postulated also brings in the idea of the New Untouchables—the democrats in general.

What the Indian fascists are doing is through its attack on the "corrupt" Congress Party (rather it should be "unclean" and "impure" Congress Party according to the fascist imaginary), is re-drafting the caste markers: pure/impure, high/low, clean/unclean, corrupt/uncorrupt into the new spaces for political action in 2014. What the RSS is thus doing is to put the Congress Party and the entire bourgeois democratic tradition as the unclean and corrupt other (or to borrow Sartre's term the "hellish other"). One has literally to purify India (Savarkar's fictitious "holy land") and thereby cleanse India by attacking the Congress. Remember for the RSS the crimes or rather sins of the Congress emerge from their subscription to the ideologies of secularism and socialism. For the RSS the secularists and socialists are untouchables. And as we shall see, for the Congress, it is the Communists that are untouchables, people who are as Sonia Gandhi just said trapped in the ideology of the 19th century ("a party sticks to ideology that became irrelevant"), as if the liberals and the fascists in their ode to "Indian tradition" are living in the 21st century!

What Indian fascism under Modi will do is that it will let neo-liberalism attack workers' rights while simultaneously letting the Congress attack the Communists. But what fascism will do the most is to fuzz up the caste hierarchy—after all is Modi not the "*chaiwalla*", the son of the OBC proletariat?—and in doing so also try to bring not only the OBCs into the bandwagon of fascism but also renegade Dalit leaders like Ramdas Athawale and Ram Vilas Paswan. But this fascist logic is built on the liberal logic of concealment where the fiction of "Dalit capitalism" is created. What is not understood is that this form of Dalit capitalism will not transform the untouchables into democratic citizens, but primarily brush under the carpet the complete project of Dalit liberation in particular and human emancipation in general.

From the Hindu Rashtra as Psychotic Symptom of Late Capitalism to Hindutva as Total Fascism

We thus unleash a certain kind of fury that envelopes many movements for social and political emancipation. The fury is directed to the exploiters, the counterrevolutionaries, the communal-fascists, the capitalists and imperialist cartels. But the fury is also directed towards the hidden ideologists and the wielders of the ideology-of-dominance, an ideology-of-dominance that has led not only to a type of ideological blindness, but also to a silent counterrevolution in India. This silent counterrevolution has been blind to the question of caste and then constructed an imaginary theme of India being a Hindu society. Our claim is that this silent counterrevolution has *restrained the human mind within the smallest compass*, creating organized superstition, and depriving the Indian people of "all grandeur and historical energies"[34], to not only the inherent social structures of India, but also the imperialist policies of

Washington-based think-tanks.

What we claim is that in the complete overhauling of the entire ideological superstructure of capitalism, the complete overhauling of the caste system and the ideological myth of Hinduism is absolutely necessary. One cannot work without the other. It is not merely that we argue against imperialism, as if imperialism exists independent of pre-capitalist social formations. One needs to link organically the relation between global capital accumulation, the Indian elites and the ideology of dominance in India. The organic linking of the relation between the economic base of accumulation of capital and the superstructure of mass hysteria (of: "We are Hindus being swamped by Pakistanis and Bangladeshis in our own homeland") and the corresponding stratification, superstition and backwardness needs to be studied.

One needs to link the Yankee War Industry and the Indian ideology-in-dominance. One also needs to point out the rise of fascism in India and the role of caste and imperialism in the emergence of fascism. One thus needs to claim that even the so-called holy book of Hinduism which now the RSS wants to promote as the "national book" is not in any way to be confused with any sort of philosophical or ethical treatise. One needs to deny the moral claims of the *Gita* as it does nothing but represent the ideological upholding of the caste system. One needs also to emphasize alongside Ambedkar that the claim that the *Gita* is devoid of any message is absolutely correct.[35] And what Ambedkar calls the ideology of the "justification of war" and "a philosophical defence of war and killing in war"[36] that the *Gita* advocates is directly related to the ideology of wars and riots that the RSS actively preaches. The classical book for the Indian counterrevolution[37], as Ambedkar calls the *Gita,* now has metamorphosized into the RSS fascist manual of taking absolute power in India.

Yet it must be noted that the contemporary version of fascism in India is backed by corporate capitalism and takes on a more lethal form than the one that emerged in the Ram Janmabhoomi-Babri Masjid movement. This does not imply that the early project (Ram Janmabhoomi-Babri Masjid movement) has been sidelined for an imagined development type of fascism, where just as Mussolini is said to have made the trains run on time, so too Narendra Modi is going to do the same.

To strike at the Ideological State Apparatus (now being monopolized by the communal-fascists and supported globally by the American-led corporate imperialism), one needs to articulate how this Ideological State Apparatus produces not only this "hysterical melancholia" that Walter Benjamin talked of, but now produces what we call after Fredric Jameson as the *'hysterical sublime"*.[38] There are two productions here in the ideology of the sublime. One that creates the early liberal discourse of Hinduism (from Vivekananda to Gandhi—this version has aesthetics within its cranium), and the second sort of sublime is a fascist version where the sublime has nothing to do with aesthetics. Instead this second version of the sublime destroys all capacities of human thinking and instead gives way to hysteria. This passage we call: *the passage from the sublime to hysteria*. And it is this passage that the fascists have mastered. *The hysterical sublime crushes all desire for revolution.*

So what is this hysterical sublime and how is fascism related to it? In my *The New Militants* I have talked of the production of this hysterical sublime. Let us have a look at it. It is on the one hand "the experience bordering on terror, the fitful glimpse, in astonishment, stupor and awe of what was so enormous as to crush life altogether".[39] It is also "the limit of figuration and the incapacity of the human mind to give representation".[40] But basically it is a "phantasmatic relationship with some organic pre-capitalist peasant landscape and village society".[41] In this phantasmatic representation, the mass hysteria of "being Hindu" implies a phantasy created by some sort of castration anxiety which is projected elsewhere (i.e. the production of the "Hindu" as the one who is crushed by the "Muslim"). This mass hysteria is also the master signifier of the Indian culture industry where people who are unhappy in the unhappy home of capitalism are served with this sense of false happiness. This hysterical sublime is thus what once Marx called *the feeling of ease and strength in human self-estrangement*.[42] One is thus forced to say with cynicism and irony: caste has never left us. Like Freud's eternal recurrence of the neurotic, caste returns to haunt us once again.

"Dalit Capitalism", the Indian State and the New Untouchables

What the RSS type of fascism will do in its attempt to mobilize Dalits and other marginalized groups is that it shall cover the caste system with the blanket of hysterical blindness, thus postulating an imaginary "Hindu" community devoid of caste. But its aim is not merely to incorporate the Dalits into their apparatus, but incorporate them to be used against secularism and democracy. It will thus try to incorporate sections of Dalits, tribals and OBCs in their various paraphernalia, while building a fascist state mechanism and appearing to attack liberal democracy (here the Congress Party).

What one has to do is de-mystify the relation of the fascist RSS with Dalits and other subaltern groups. But in this de-mystification of fascist illusions one also has to de-mystify the liberal imaginary of capitalism emancipating the Dalits. Recall Lenin's understanding of liberals as civilized hyenas who "whet their teeth on Asia" and liberalism "rotten within" that tries to revive itself in the form of "socialist *opportunism*".[43] What one needs to do is not only attack "Hinduism" as the culture of pre-capitalism in India, but also actively attack liberalism in the attack on fascism. *One cannot tie up with liberals and social opportunists in the struggle against fascism.*

And since the New Illusion of "Dalit capitalism" is created by a motley crowd comprising sections of the big bourgeoisie, neo-liberal economists and members of both liberal and fascist parties, it is also necessary to de-mystify the illusion of "Dalit capitalism", while de-mystifying the phantasmagoria of Hinduism. It must be noted that capitalism always creates a large section of the Industrial Reserve Army (what Marcuse called the "Great Refusal") while claiming to be democratic. And that is why one must also say that liberal capitalism will make claims of inclusion (does not Rahul Gandhi say this in his meetings???) and equality, it will primarily be based on real inequality (the inequality between capital and labour).

While the question of the "untouchables" as the excluded other being sociologically placed in the site of casteism is best understood in Ambedkar's radical theory, the philosophical critique of exclusion is best understood in Marx's theory of alienation that deconstructs the extreme borders of cruelty. What we know now (made fashionable by contemporary academic sociology) as the discourses of exclusion is in actuality based in the very serious site of Marx's theory of alienation. One knows that at least since 1844 with Marx's *Economic and Philosophic Manuscripts of 1844* this theory of alienation entered radical critical theory, despite the structuralist critic of this theory as exemplified by the works of Louis Althusser. This very strange forgetfulness of Marx's theory of alienation has blunted the radical politics of Revolutionary Marxism which forgot Marx's historicism and humanism for a bland theory (one should say theory converted to theology) of historical evolutionarism. One knows that Gramsci and Lukács had critiqued this form of anti-humanism within the left movement.

Locating the question of the politics of exclusion and the political "untouchables" in the field of alienation is now the urgent task that we need to perform. In more than one sense one can locate the period after the 1857 war of independence against the British Raj as holding the manifold contradictions from which both the idea of the modern Indian state as well as the many types of reactionary nationalist ideologies developed, many of them having within them the political logic of exclusion in the early bourgeois era. Now it is both well known and well documented that the primary ideological contradiction as spelt out by the contemporary neo-Hindu right was the spurious opposition between the imagined "good Hindu" vs. the even more imagined "bad Muslim". The fact that this form of neo-fascist ideology has seeped so deep in contemporary India, with the help of imperialist Islamophobia, that one needs to rearticulate Marx's theory of alienation for contemporary times. Liberalism has done nothing to confront Islamophobia, has done nothing to confront the politics of Hindutva. All the liberals are interested in is worshipping at the feet of the Towers of the World Bank.

Turn to contemporary times and recall the previous Prime Minister (Manmohan Singh) landing in England in 2005 and literally telling the imperialist government of the Brits that their role as colonialists in India was not only progressive, but literally to be celebrated. Turn now to the discourses of the Neo-Adam Smiths in India (Chandra Bhan Prasad, an ex-Maoist is one of the proponents of this fiction) which talk of "Dalit capitalism", a form of phantasmagorical version of capitalism that is pure fiction, a fiction devoid of the bloody history of primitive accumulation, devoid of what we know since David Harvey as "accumulation through dispossession". Remember that for this form of neo-liberal sponsored fiction, we now do not talk of "victimhood", we "don't ask for doles, reservations, favours... (and) complains".[44] Instead of the struggle of the oppressed, a struggle that is between master and slave—rather lordship and bondage—(a struggle as in Hegel's *Phenomenology of Mind* where lordship is bound to be overthrown), the oppressed are seen as Chandra Bhan Prasad claims, to have "risen on their own".[45] The struggle of the oppressed has "outlived its potential and power", as the ex-Maoist, turned neo-liberal claims.[46] That this neo-liberal narrative echoes the narrative that India is the subordinate partner of American imperialism should be stressed. That Dalit capitalism is made up of small and medium enterprises based largely on family labour, and subservient to the needs of big capital also should not be forgotten. This reflects the Brahmanical 10th Mandala, where the Dalits (even as imaginary Dalit capitalists) remain as the feet of the upper caste big bourgeoisie.

It should be noted that Ratan Tata and Adi Godrej are mentioned by the pioneers of "Dalit capitalism". Chandra Bhan Prasad forgets that "Dalit capitalism" is both a commodity (needed by the Tatas and the Godrejs to produce the spare parts for these global magnates) as well as a spectacle. Chandra Bhan Prasad also forgets that the Tatas and the Godrejs do not belong to the clan of the varna fetish worshippers, but belong to a faith that has been diametrically opposed to caste and Brahmanism for well over two and a half millennia. Thus while equality (albeit only formal equality) is possible for faiths other that Hinduism, it is impossible for Hinduism to accept any form of equality. Yet the proponents of "Dalit capitalism" like the proponents of "Islamic capitalism" (many who are friends of Narendra Modi) forget that capitalism both sweeps the remnants of pre-capitalist societies, as well as re-imagines and re-builds these same primordial social formations. Therefore Rosa Luxemburg's argument that there can be no neat picture of capitalism devoid of pre-capitalism and that capitalism needs pre-capitalist societies for the realization of surplus value is of great importance.

And since this neo-liberal narrative blames Marx for not understanding that capitalism does sweep pre-capitalist societies with brutal force, it must be stated that the neo-liberals have not even bothered to read Marx, forget able to understand him. Consider the dialectical and critical reading of history by Marx and Engels. It must be noted that while on the one hand certain forms of pre-capitalism are retained by the storm of capital accumulation, there is another part where capitalism sweeps anything that comes in its way creating a world after its own brutal image. This dual role of capitalism—destroying pre-capitalist social formations and retaining them should be contextualized in the two stages of capitalism: the earlier revolutionary stage and the later decadent stage. Consider Marx and Engels:

> The bourgeoisie, historically, has played a most revolutionary part. The bourgeoisie, wherever it has got the upper hand, has put an end to all feudal, patriarchcal, idyllic relations. It has pitilessly torn asunder the motley feudal ties that bound man to his "natural superiors," and has left remaining no other nexus between human and human than naked self-interest, than callous "cash payment." It has drowned the most heavenly ecstasies (*die heilogen Schauer*) of religious fervour, of chivalrous enthusiasm (*der ritterlichen Begeisterung*), of philistine sentimentalism (*der spiessburgerlichen Wehmuth*), in the icy water of egotistical calculation (*egoistischen Berechnung*). It has resolved personal worth into exchange value, and in place of the numberless indefeasible chartered freedoms, has set up that single, unconscionable freedom — Free Trade. In one word, for exploitation, veiled by religious and political illusions, it has substituted naked, shameless, direct, brutal exploitation.
>
> The bourgeoisie has stripped of its halo every occupation hitherto honoured and looked up to with reverent awe. It has converted the physician, the lawyer, the priest, the poet, the man of science, into its paid wage labourers.
>
> The bourgeoisie has torn away from the family its sentimental veil, and has reduced the family relation to a mere money relation.
>
> The bourgeoisie has disclosed how it came to pass that the brutal display of vigour in the Middle Ages, which reactionaries so much admire, found its fitting complement in the most slothful indolence. It has been the first to show what man's activity can bring about. It has accomplished wonders far surpassing Egyptian pyramids, Roman aqueducts, and Gothic cathedrals; it has conducted expeditions that put in the shade all former Exoduses of nations and crusades.
>
> The bourgeoisie cannot exist without constantly revolutionizing the instruments of production, and thereby the relations of production, and with them the whole relations of society.

> Conservation of the old modes of production in unaltered form, was, on the contrary, the first condition of existence for all earlier industrial classes. Constant revolutionizing of production, uninterrupted disturbance of all social conditions, everlasting uncertainty and agitation distinguish the bourgeois epoch from all earlier ones. All fixed, fast-frozen relations, with their train of ancient and venerable prejudices and opinions, are swept away, all new-formed ones become antiquated before they can ossify. All that is solid melts into air, all that is holy is profaned, and man is at last compelled to face with sober senses his real conditions of life, and his relations with his kind.
>
> The need of a constantly expanding market for its products chases the bourgeoisie over the entire surface of the globe. It must nestle everywhere, settle everywhere, establish connexions everywhere.[47]

One will however have to re-contextualize the passage in the era of rising fascism: "It (capitalism) has drowned the most heavenly ecstasies of religious fervour, of chivalrous enthusiasm (*der ritterlichen Begeisterung*), of philistine sentimentalism (*der spiessburgerlichen Wehmuth*), in the icy water of egotistical calculation" into a new light that sees this insane chivalry of feudalism returning once again. With regards the translation: "chivalrous enthusiasm" (*der ritterlichen Begeisterung*), it needs to be stated that *ritterlichen* could be "chivalrous", but this "chivalry" is intrinsically related to "knightly" that is inherent in Marx's idea of feudal Europe. This same phrase: *der ritterlichen Begeisterung* is also related to Marx's idea of Don Quixote, the ideal idyllic-feudal. Marx here means that the revolutionary bourgeoisie "drowned" this "knightly inspiration" (my translation) or "chivalrous enthusiasm" (the standard translation) and "heavenly ecstasies" (*die heilogen Schauer*) of feudalism into "egotistical calculation" (*egoistischen Berechnung*). What happens in India is that capitalism would not completely destroy pre-capitalist social formations, but would incorporate these ancient caste-communities into modern capitalism. The ghosts of the chivalrous Don Quixotes of pre-capitalist India would return as the not so chivalrous Narendra Modi.

What we are doing now is changing the phrase: "the most heavenly ecstasies of religious fervour, of chivalrous enthusiasm (*der ritterlichen Begeisterung*) and philistine sentimentalism (*der spiessburgerlichen Wehmuth*)" being drowned "in the icy water of egotistical calculation" into the new phrase: *chivalrous enthusiasm and philistine sentimentalism are mixed with egotistical calculation*. What we are doing is transforming the term: "philistine sentimentalism" (*der spiessburgerlichen Wehmuth*) into the new term: "bourgeois (or philistine) melancholy".[48] The translation: "sentimentalism" could be innocent, if not totally wrong, especially with Narendra Modi around. The word "*Wehmuth*" indicates a form of woefulness or melancholy, which if I am not mistaken Walter Benjamin brings in his works. That Benjamin talks of this melancholy in the era of rising fascism ought not to be missed. What the fascists are best at doing is able to manipulate the process of melancholy.

Two things happen: (1) that fascism appears with the technique of manipulating melancholia, and (2) neo-liberalism and the liberals forget history totally. The politics of the neo-liberals is vulgar to the extreme. When Chandra Bhan Prasad tells Shekhar Gupta that "Montek (i.e. Montek Singh Ahluwalia) is a friend of Adam Smith and Adam Smith is an enemy of Manu, so therefore, Montek is our friend"[49], and one must shift one's ideal from Mao to Obama, then one needs to state that if in any possible way the Indian neo-liberal wants to imitate the history of American capitalism and imperialism. One also wants to know what Prasad did when the 2006 Khairilanji massacre happened and when Dalit activists are being arrested as terrorists. The neo-liberals want to be consciously blind to real history, especially blind to the threat of fascism.

But one needs to stress the most, is that not only is Ambedkar's original philosophy of annihilation of caste conveniently forgotten in the blindness to the threat of fascism and for the lust of the fetishism of commodities, but one also needs to stress that in this phantasmagorical narrative how the Indian liberal state has called one section of the radical left the "single biggest threat to Indian internal security". In other words, one must try to understand how the Indian liberals are totally oblivious to fascism and fixated against Revolutionary Communism. That the radical left is being stamped by the Indian state as the "New Untouchables" is a sign post that the Indian state is moving to fascism with (what we say with great irony and contempt) the *"peaceful transformation from liberalism to fascism"*.

This is the new battle front of the "New Untouchables". And in this new battle front one needs to de-think Indian ideology: from the 10th Mandala of the *Rg Veda* and Manu to Gandhi, Savarkar, the neo-liberals and the Indian fascists. And it is in this process of de-thinking the entire "Indian ideology" (if we may be permitted to borrow this phrase from Perry Anderson) that the struggle between lordship and bondage must be fought out.

The battle against Indian fascism is simultaneously a battle against this "Indian ideology" that begins with the *Rg Veda* and ends via Manu with the various chambers of commerce wherein roams the ghosts of the Indian fascists seen with holy ashes smeared on their not so holy brows.

REFERENCES

1. Walter Benjamin, 'The Work of Art in the Age of Mechanical Reproduction', in *Illuminations,* trans. Harry Zohn (Glasgow: Fontana/Collins, 1979), p. 226.
2. Ibid., p. 243.
3. Walter Benjamin said that: "This is the situation of politics which fascism is rendering aesthetic. Communism responds by politicizing art". Ibid., p. 244.
4. See Jairus Banaji, 'Fascism as a Mass Movement: Translator's Introduction', and Arthur Rosenberg, 'Fascism as a Mass Movement', in Jairus Banaji, *Fascism: Essays on Europe and India* (New Delhi: Three Essays Collective, 2013).

5. B.R. Ambedkar, 'Annihilation of Caste', in *The Essential Writings of B.R. Ambedkar*, ed. Valerian Rodrigues (New Delhi: Oxford University Press, 2008), p. 273.
6. Wendy Doniger, *On Hinduism* (New Delhi: Aleph Book Company, 2013), pp. 126-41
7. Ibid., pp. 426-37.
8. B.R. Ambedkar, 'Annihilation of Caste', p. 275.
9. Jyoti Phule, 'Cultivator's Whipcord', in *Selected Writings of Jotirao Phule*, ed. G.P. Deshpande (New Delhi: LeftWord, 2010), pp. 120, 122.
10. Wendy Doniger, *On Hinduism*, p. 126.
11. Karl Marx, 'A Contribution to the Critique of Hegel's Philosophy of Right. Introduction', in *Karl Marx. Early Writings*, trans. Rodney Livingstone and Gregor Benton (London: Penguin, 1992), p. 243.
12. B.R. Ambedkar, 'Annihilation of Caste', p. 267.
13. Ibid., p. 274.
14. Karl Marx, 'The British Rule in India, in *Marx. Engels. On Colonialism* (Moscow: Progress Publishers, 1976), p. 40.
15. Karl Marx *Capital*, Vol. I, trans. Samuel Moore and Eduard Aveling (Moscow: Progress Publishers, 1983), p. 321
16. Slavoj Žižek, 'A Plea for Leninist Intolerance', in *Critical Inquiry*, Winter, 2002.
17. B.R. Ambedkar, The Failures of Parliamentary Democracy', in *Thus Spoke Ambedkar. Volume 1. A Stake in the Nation* (ed.) Bhagwan Das (New Delhi: Navayana, 2010), p. 46.
18. See my *The New Militants* (Delhi: Aakar Books, 2014) for an entirely different rendering of the "new militants" who critique liberal democracy and caste.
19. Karl Marx *Capital*, Vol. I, p. 338-9
20. See Karl Marx, 'First Draft of Reply to V.Z. Zasulich's Letter', in *Karl Marx. Frederick Engels, Selected Works*, Vol. 3 (Moscow: Progress Publishers, 1977), pp. 152-61.
21. D.D. Kosambi, *The Culture and Civilization of Ancient India in Historical Outline* (New Delhi: Vikas Publishing House, 2000), pp. 15-6.
22. Ibid., p. 17.
23. B.R. Ambedkar, 'Annihilation of Caste', in *The Essential Writings of B.R. Ambedkar*, ed. Valerian Rodrigues (New Delhi: Oxford University Press, 2008), p. 267.
24. See Richard King, *Orientalism and the Myth of Modern Hinduism* (New Delhi: Critical Quest, 2008), p. 14.
25. See David Lorenzen, 'Who Invented Hinduism?' in *Society for*

Comparative Study of Society and History, 1999.

26. Wendy Doniger, op. cit., p. 147.
27. Ibid., p. 144.
28. Karl Marx, *Das Kapital*, Erster Band (Berlin: Dietz Verlag, 1981), p. 52.
29. B.R. Ambedkar, 'Annihilation of Caste', in *The Essential Writings of B.R. Ambedkar*, p. 267.
30. See my 'Why We Are Not Hindus: A Reply to the Indian Fascists', in *Mainstream*, Vol. LII, No. 1, December 28, 2013, p. 110.
31. Quoted in Romila Thapar, *Past and Prejudice* (National Book Trust: New Delhi, 1993), p. 12.
32. Ibid.
33. Ibid., pp. 14-5.
34. Karl Marx, 'The British Rule in India', in *On Colonialism* (Moscow: Progress Publishers, 1976), pp. 40-41.
35. B.R. Ambedkar, 'Krishna and His Gita', in *The Essential Writings of B.R. Ambedkar*, p. 193.
36. Ibid.
37. Ibid., pp. 195-7.
38. Fredric Jameson, *Postmodernism or the Cultural Logic of Late Capitalism* (London: Verso, 1991), p. 14.
39. Ibid.
40. Ibid.
41. Ibid.
42. Karl Marx and Frederick Engels, *The Holy Family* (Moscow: Progress Publishers, 1980), p. 46.
43. V.I. Lenin, 'The Historical Destiny of the Doctrine of Karl Marx', in *Lenin. Selected Works* (Moscow: Progress Publishers, 1975), pp. 18-9.
44. 'Capitalism is Changing Caste Much Faster Than Any Human Being. Dalits Should Look at Capitalism as a Crusader Against Caste', in *Indian Express*, June 11, 2013.
45. Ibid.
46. Ibid.
47. Karl Marx and Frederick Engels, 'Manifesto of the Communist Party', in *Marx. Engels. Selected Works* (Moscow: Progress Publishers, 1975), pp. 37-8.
48. I must thank Arun Patnaik for making me think on this passage.
49. See 'Capitalism is Changing Caste Much Faster Than Any Human Being. Dalits Should Look at Capitalism as a Crusader Against Caste', in *Indian Express*, June 11, 2013.

6

Education and the Anti-Fascist Revolution

All educational work in the field in the Soviet Republic of Workers and Peasants, in the field of political education in general and in the field of art in particular, should be imbued with the spirit of the class struggle being waged by the proletariat for the successful achievement of the aims of the dictatorship of the proletariat, i.e. the overthrow of the bourgeoisie, the abolition of all classes, and the elimination of all forms of exploitation of man by man.

V.I. Lenin

Everybody is already cultured.

Antonio Gramsci

Schools are prison houses.

Ivan Ilich

Why is the educational system so rarely subjugated to radical criticism?

Pierre Bourdieu

On Fascist Techno-clerics

What one needs to do is to go directly to the masses. One will now have to create what Lenin once called "dual power" where revolutionaries will have to dig in their trenches to commence firstly the war of position (Gramcsi's "passive revolution"). In this first stage, one will first have to tell the masses that the clear cut opposition that Rosa Luxemburg had shown as the opposition between barbarism and socialism is primarily between the ideology of Manu and that of Ambedkar. The question is very simply put: *fascism or democracy?* And since nothing called "democratic fascism" ever existed, one will have to retrieve both the idea of democracy, as well as the idea of India.

Despite there being nothing called "democratic fascism", the present government insists that they are democratic fascists. They want people's opinions. Of course when they stopped the livelihood of Muslims by banning beef and declaring that even possessing beef is a crime, they did not ask for opinions. But out of the blue the government is asking for opinions in formulating a new educational policy. And since they ask for an opinion, we shall give ours to them. We shall talk to them about their favourite topic—history. Unfortunately this also is a topic of great importance for both Marx and Ambedkar. Louis Althusser had said that Marx had discovered a new continent of knowledge—history, or to be precise historical materialism, just as before there were two continents of knowledge discovered—mathematics and physics.[1] We shall see that there are different types of histories: tragic, farcical, comic, pathological and extremely joyous.

While history throughout the world follows the path of development, history in India, it seems, follows a circular and repetitive path, like Freud's neurotic compulsion to repeat. Let us see how this neurotic appears in the present government department. Quite recently the Ministry for Human Resource Development (MHRD) asked for people's suggestions in formulating a New Educational Policy for India. This seems like a joke that has turned into tragedy and a tragedy that has turned into a joke. And considering that the ruling political establishment after declaring a million times over that India is a "Hindu Rashtra", is once again attempting to declare this jocular-tragedy for the million and one time, one needs to think aloud: is this New Education Policy anything to do with their terrible fascist ambition of turning secular and democratic India into a fascist state? And considering that this same establishment has discovered the glorious wisdom of the even more glorious Indian past, one wonders what the people of India need to learn and what this New Education Policy will do. Or may be since it is felt that wisdom (both ancient and modern) is lost, one will have to contact the lost-and-found department in some state bureaucracy to formulate a New Education Policy.

But to this dilemma, it is modern capitalism that comes to the rescue of this tragicomic New Education Policy, not to forget also to the service of India's not-so-glorious glorious past and the ruling political establishment. At one point one has capitalism creating the literal lust for commodities and the accumulation of capital which needs modern science and technology. And for that education as technocratic education is necessary. What one produces from these massive industries of education are technocrats and clerks or what one may call "techno-clerks" whose sole role is producing commodities and rendering unnecessary real philosophical and scientific thinking.

Now considering that the new political order in India is not merely going to mimic the old soft-Hindutva political order of Atal Bihari Vajpayee, but going to create a totalitarian administrative neo-liberal state that obliterates all dissent (built on the models of Zionist Israel and the Islamic Republic of Iran), one needs to think and think quickly what the MHRD is planning to do with education. What would this ministry do? Would it neatly divide society into two halves: on the one side these strange techno-clerks along with the seekers of ancient wisdom and on the other side large parts of the Indian population that will be put under the jackboots of these fascist *techno-clerics*? Thus would we have not merely the rule of the techno-clerks but the governance of techno-clerics like in contemporary Iran? It must be noted that both the RSS and the Iranian mullahs share a very strong ideological bondage—both are fiercely anti-secularist and both imagine that messianic clerks will rescue humanity. But both are primarily products of industrial capitalism whose violence they seek to justify and promote. Both are advocates of symbolic violence. And both, of course, love Adolf Hitler.

Need of a Subaltern Indian Renaissance

The rather sad state of affairs lies in the fact that the Indian elites, right from the time of independence, were seduced by capitalism which drew the Indian populace into misery and poverty. The recent triumph of the Indian fascists lies in the brute fact of capitalism, the misery that it produced and the dystopian hopes that it generates. And since the Indian fascists have transformed this misery and dystopia into hysteria, one can only expect hysterical misery in India.

At the level of the educational superstructure this sad state of hysterical miserable affairs in India lies in the fact that the Indian Renaissance and Enlightenment have not been understood, forget them being realized. And because the Indian Renaissance and Enlightenment were not understood and because India's modern education system grew from the cranium of the Orientalists that was realized in British colonial policy that divided the population of India into warring religious groups: Hindu, Muslim, Christians, etc; and also because the colonial census of 1872 further classified the people of India in terms of caste; the very idea of "Indian people" and consequently "Indian people's education" remained only on paper. Because of these two flaws that repressed the development of an "Indian people's education system" and also because the elites managed to control education where education (at least since the last two decades) has been treated merely as a commodity and not a national necessity; the Indian population was further divided into two large economic groups: the educated elites (with the technocrats serving the global IT sector) and the undereducated (and even totally illiterate) subaltern masses. What further happened in the last two decades was that the humanities and the social sciences were devalued and a great hype was created in favour of the technical sciences. What then happened was a new caste system that evolved where we got (as Gopal Guru had informed us) "theoretical Brahmans" (the doctors, technicians, natural scientists) and the "empirical Shudras" (the practitioners of humanities and the social sciences). The working populace would be the ati-Shudras—completely out of sight from national imagination. The modern education system, with its exam-centric orientation, would not give knowledge or decrease class and caste differences (something which Amartya Sen and Jean Dreze think it to be), but on the contrary would reproduce the class nature of society (as Pierre Bourdieu rightly theorized). Education in this sense would be a sense of enslavement. It would continuously produce and reproduce hierarchies and power structures. One here recalls Bourdieu:

> The School, this privileged instrument of the bourgeois sociodicy which confers on the privileged the supreme privilege of not seeing themselves as privileged, manages the more easily to convince the disinherited that they owe their scholastic and social destiny to their lack of gifts or merits, because in matters of culture absolute dispossession excludes awareness of being dispossessed.[2]

What one suggests is that a complete inversion and overhauling of education needs being done with the idea of toiling humanity and the Indian people kept at the centre of its national educational programme. This programme starts from primary education where it develops a detailed programme for school education where not only are the above stated divisions totally obliterated, but also where a humanist theory of education is developed where not only are the natural and social sciences united, but also where aesthetics (from drama, painting and poetry to music) and ethics play a fundamental role in education.

Yet education does not exist by itself, just as "development" does not exist by itself. It has as its core humanity and thus those who talk of "development" without mentioning that this "development" that the Indian state is now talking of is only brutal capitalist development (or accumulation through dispossession that is destroying humanity); one is only talking through the air. Instead of this airy talk one has to put forward an anti-capitalist programme that is both real and practical. One has to take a look back at the first years of India's independence and one sees not the neo-liberal policies that the state is now harping on, but something quite different where the welfare state envisaged a dire need for universal education and health *for all* in India. But this "all" fell to the miseries of capitalism and an aborted independence. They got neither education nor health. And since this "all" is now to be controlled by mega-corporations, one begins by quoting Rabindranath Tagore (who recently has been recalled by Amartya Sen and Jean Dreze): "The imposing tower of misery which today rests on the heart of India has its sole foundation in the absence of education".[3] To convert this absence of education residing in the tower of misery to the possibilities and necessities of universal education is the main point of this document. Yet, we must state, right at the beginning, our philosophy of education is not uncritical. It does not borrow blindly from the ideologies of education set forth by industrialized society.

The leitmotiv of making a document of people's education policy is based on understanding the tension and opposition between the idea of education as instruction and education as cultivation of humanity as humanity. The idea of the *historicization and humanization* of knowledge is the essence of this education programme. The triad of science, philosophy and the arts serves as the methodological basis of this Educational Programme. According to this programme by "science" one means the exploration and understanding of the laws governing nature and society[4], by "philosophy" one means the method of emancipatory knowing where the proletariat educates its class instincts and by "arts" one means the study of the sublime and the beautiful. To create the sublime feeling of enthusiasm is the main part of this programme.

It is thus that we claim that a people's education document is based on the understanding of education as cultivation of the human mind.[5] But it is not merely the cultivation of the mind that is important, but the cultivation of humanity as humanity. Its starting point is philosophical: its main questions are: "What can humanity know?", "what can humanity do?", "what can humanity hope for?"[6] and "how can free humanity be truly possible?" The modern principles of liberty, equality and fraternity are its guiding principles. Challenging educational orthodoxy is its leitmotiv. De-schooling society is its essence, since schools have become the prison-houses and panoptic systems that imprison young minds. To render the necessity of critical thinking is its motto. Philosophy, science and aesthetics are its three basic epistemological components. Perception, understanding and reason along with feeling, willing and desiring are its ontological components. As Marx had once said: *let us produce according to the laws of beauty*.[7] The critique of human alienation and the commoditization of education are its important concerns. Not only the critique of alienation in modern capitalist India, but also the critique of alienation in traditional caste-based society, combined with alienation in centres of learning (schools, colleges and universities) shall be forms of communist programmatic concerns.

The following points are important in the scientific, philosophizing and aestheticization of education:

(1) Education as cultivation of humanity is the culmination of the Subaltern Indian Renaissance. But this Indian Renaissance is a Renaissance "from below". It therefore follows the subaltern logic of class struggle. It studies humanity as humanity (free from

superstitions, free from semi-feudal values, free from caste and patriarchy, free from communal hatred, free from scarcity and want and free from the capitalism mode of production). As the culmination of the Indian Renaissance "from below", it talks of a New Humanism for India. Cultural transformation is the main point in this programme of Communist New Humanism.

(2) It follows the research methodology of historical dialectics where science is seen as a unified science. Here neither are the different branches of the social sciences split from one another, nor are the natural sciences split from the social sciences. It sees the unity of the natural and the social sciences since it sees the unity of nature and society. Its method is human natural science also known as the natural science of humanity[8], where social history as natural history[9] is marked as its leitmotiv. By science we do not mean a form of scientism or positivism. Instead we have something very different:

> History itself is a real part of *natural history*—of nature developing into humanity. Natural science will in time incorporate into itself the science of humanity, just as the science of humanity will incorporate into itself natural science: there will be *one* science.[10]

Science here, in the very Marxist humanist sense, does not merely study facts, but as *human natural sciences* unites facts and ethics. It always sees the human basis of facts. The humanization and naturalization of knowledge and education is thus its philosophical premise. What human natural science does is that it critiques the dominant methods of education that have been borrowed from colonialism. The critique of Eurocentrism (the method that claims that the West is inherently endowed with reason, while the rest of the world can only develop on borrowed European and American methods, a model that is the basis of the neo-liberal political economy of globalization, a political economy which the new establishment strongly believes in) and the critique of the colonization of education find its place in this process of the humanization of education. Thus this critique of Eurocentrism is also coupled with the critique of the indigenous colonization (known as "Brahmanization") of education. The New Indian Renaissance finds two sites of the colonization of the Indian mind: Eurocentrism and Brahmanism. While we involve the method of humanization of knowledge, we also set up different interventions within the domain of a general theory of humanist education where Schiller's *On the Aesthetic Education of Humanity*, the Hegelian dialectical method, the Marxist critique of capitalism, Jyotiba Phule's theory and praxis of *"manuski"* (humanist) education, along with B.R. Ambedkar's programme of the annihilation of caste (and semi-feudal values) is taken as its motif. Thus the best that world education has to offer shall be taken.

(3) With these principles of the New Indian Renaissance and human natural science, the role of education as a weapon that grips the masses comes up. Education as the cultivation of the human mind and as the study of knowledge links this scientific enterprise with developing societies. The critique of pre-capitalist forms of exploitation (wrongly christened "Indian feudalism") and neo-liberalism finds its place here. A rethinking of Indian history from the perspective of the Asiatic mode of production where caste, communal-fascism and patriarchy along with economic and cultural underdevelopment is undertaken in the production of the Renaissance "from below". The philosophical and scientific foundations of the annihilation of caste, communal antagonisms and patriarchy are laid in this paradigm of the New Indian Renaissance.

(4) From this we deduce the political economy of underdevelopment where the centre and periphery of globalized capitalism's accumulation of wealth is scientifically critiqued. Both the economic and cultural dependency of India on borrowed colonial models is reviewed.

(5) This critique of the colonization of the mind is not based on the ideology of abstract intellectualism. Instead it unites the intellect and the will, thinking and feeling. It is consequently based on what is now being called "*synesthesia*" or the "union of the senses". The leitmotiv of this project of *synesthesia* is philosophical, in the sense it will seek the groundwork of knowledge based on the question: "How is free humanity possible?" It thus seeks the groundwork for the possibilities of free humanity. What we mean by "education" is consequently based on the above premises. G.W.F. Hegel's theory of dialectical logic, Marx's critique of alienation and his reworking of Ludwig Feuerbach's idea of "species being", Gramsci's theory of the organic intellectual, J.P. Naik's theory of understanding education as a Revolution with a Revolution, Ivan Illich's idea of de-schooling society and Paulo Friere and Pierre Bourdieu's ideas of bourgeois education as cultural subjugation shall be the guiding principles of a people's education policy. The idea of challenging educational orthodoxy is the leitmotiv of this programme.

(6) Understanding this challenging of educational orthodoxy impels us to articulate the role played by material labour in this New Cultural Transformation. In this materialist ontology of labour a different understanding of India's social history is seen where the Asiatic mode of production is articulated along

with the traditional Asian craft and guild system from an anti-Brahmanical perspective. In this critique of Brahmanism one documents the labour movement in India. One also documents how the false division of people as pure and clean (the Brahmans) and unclean and impure (the Shudras), along with the false construction of Brahmanical rituals as "spiritual sciences" and the consequent spurious division of the "spiritual sciences" and the "indigenous technical-material sciences", was made since Shankara's counterrevolution against Buddhism in the 8th century C.E. What happens in this divided world is that rituals and mantras were declared true, while material sciences were declared false. This division between sacred and the profane also led to the declaration that the latter were false and also that the castes practising them were polluted and unclean. The Brahman/Shudra hostility based on the purity/pollution opposition was institutionalized since this counterrevolution. Somewhere I had said the following:

A note on Ambedkar's reading of the Hindu counterrevolution is necessary in order to place our argument in its proper context. In this little note one needs to locate Ambedkar as a Gramsciean philosopher of praxis and a Lukácsean critique of reified consciousness. A reading of caste and Hinduism as a "symbolic disorder" is based on this Gramsciean and Lukácsean critique. According to Ambedkar this infamous 'Hindu' Counterrevolution is based on two premises "graded inequality" and "division of labourers". This counterrevolution started with Adi Shankara's theological coup against the egalitarian Buddhist order and in privileging the parasitic Brahmanical priests and condemning the artisan and craftsmen as unclean untouchables. According to this type of reading, this counterrevolution privileged the infamous 'spiritualization' thesis over the indigenous sciences.[11]

But these Brahman/Shudra, material labour/spiritual labour divisions were never seriously challenged, nor was the dubious theory of the privileging the so-called "spiritual sciences" challenged, even in independent India. Both pre-colonial India as also British colonialism took this division and opposition as something natural to Indian civilization. While industrialization in India did break up the village communities, the caste system was revamped in modern lines to suit modern capitalism. The old opposition between Brahman and Shudra was transformed into the new opposition of bourgeois and proletariat. What one now needs to do is to critique both the traditional caste mode of production as also the destructive industrial model that India has undertaken as the dominant economy since independence. Our main critique is that of neo-liberalism capitalism and imperialism. This part of subaltern social history which inverts the Brahmanical and neoliberal theory of education articulates the programme of people's education. The plural and cosmopolitan understanding of Indian social history determined by the labour question shall emerge in this site.

(7) This ontology of labour now takes a new twist where a new discipline is created: the discipline of "desireology". Here education ceases to be obsessed with the mind as such. Instead it involves a paradigm shift where "ideas" are displaced for "desires". We cease to be involved with consciousness as such, but from now on education deals with the dialectic between labour, alienation and the deep unconscious. In this sense we follow Andre Breton's *First Manifesto of Surrealism* which privileged the element of the fantastic in dreams. What Marx calls the estranged

mind in the *Economic and Philosophic Manuscripts of 1844* and the phantasmagoria in *Capital* now become the main objects of educating desires, especially in the critique of neo-liberal capitalism and fascism. The synthesis of science, philosophy and the arts is now realized as a dramaturgy—the struggle against fascism. It is thus on this site that a radical critique of fascism shall emerge. Indian fascism has two parts: one that is based on the hierarchical caste system and the other which emerges from industrial capitalism. Real education has to be anti-fascist and anti-fundamentalist. Here it must be said that fascists cannot think, nor can they philosophize. They can only create mass hysteria and then destroy human civilization. True and authentic education will directly have to confront fascism. It will soon become a life and death struggle, just as neighbouring countries in South and West Asia are battling their fundamentalists and fascists.

(8) Based on the above seven points the philosophy of emancipatory praxis follows. The praxis of free-universal education emanates from this struggle against neo-liberal capitalism and fascism. We move thus from theory to praxis. The poor and wretched masses of India are the main focus of this campaign. While removal of illiteracy is its main focus, the accompanying programme of offering an alternative education to the mainstream reified types of schools is made here. We move then to forming *educational collectives*. Educational collectives de-school society from the outside. This "outside" remains literally "outside" the schools, colleges and universities at the first level, but consequently penetrates the formal educational systems, thus transforming them from hierarchical systems to systems of radical equality. It

> neither remains on the older spaces of civil society (meaning at the level of the NGOs now totally corrupted with international MNC donations attached inexorably with imperial interests) and the state (i.e. waiting for a so-called welfare or even the so-called socialist model of education, i.e. the education system that existed in the USSR). Instead educational collectives transcend both civil society and the state, and move in the New Site of the "commons". Education, i.e. true and authentic education, can only be possible when the understanding of the commons and the consequent occupation of the commons is possible. The understanding and occupation of the commons is only possible when the Subaltern Indian Renaissance is understood, started and then completed. Consequently it is imperative to differentiate the "Renaissance from above" that included the Hindu reform movement (led by Raja Rammohun Roy) and the "Renaissance from below".

The "Renaissance from above" led to Indian liberalism. Now the fascists have come. It is time for the "Renaissance from below" to speak for itself.

REFERENCES

1. Louis Althusser, *Lenin and Philosophy and Other Essays*, trans. Ben Brewster (Delhi: Aakar Books, 2006), pp. 21-3.
2. Pierre Bourdieu and Jean-Claude Passeron, *Reproduction in Education, Society and Culture* (New Delhi: Sage, 2000), p. 210.
3. Jean Dreze and Amartya Sen, *An Uncertain Glory. India and its Contradictions* (London: Allen Lane, 2013), p. 107.
4. By "science" we follow the dialectical and historical model as expounded by the philosopher G.W.F. Hegel in his *Science of Logic* where "science" is *Wissenschaft* or the seeking of real and authentic knowledge with humanity at the root of this real and

authentic knowledge. We are clearly critical of the Anglo-Saxon model of 'science' where a form of technological rationality rules the roost, a form of rationality that has totally forgotten the idea of humanity as humanity. .

5. By "mind" one means *Geist* in the sense of German Classical Philosophy which is translated as "mind" and "spirit". Knowledge production is the essence of this discourse.
7. These are three main questions for the German philosopher Immanuel Kant.
8. Karl Marx, *Economic and Philosophic Manuscripts of 1844* (Moscow: Progress Publishers, 1982), p. 69.
9. Ibid., p. 99.
10. Ibid., p. 98. Also see Karl Marx, *Capital*, Vol. I (Moscow: Progress Publishers, 1983), p. 27.
11. Karl Marx, *Economic and Philosophic Manuscripts of 1844*, p. 98.
12. See my 'Asiatic Mode of Production, Caste and the Indian Left', in *Economic & Political Weekly*, Vol. XLIX, No. 19, May 10, 2014.

Index